D0381493

The
"I Have a Life"
Dog Owner's Guide

All You Need to Be
a Fabulous Puppy Parent

Kim Campbell Thornton
and Debra Eldredge, D.V.M.

Adams Media
Avon, Massachusetts

Copyright ©2006, F+W Publications, Inc.

All rights reserved.
This book, or parts thereof, may not be reproduced in any form without permission from the publisher; exceptions are made for brief excerpts used in published reviews.

Published by Adams Media, an F+W Publications Company
57 Littlefield Street
Avon, MA 02322
www.adamsmedia.com

ISBN: 1-59337-593-X
Printed in Canada.
J I H G F E D C B A

Library of Congress Cataloging in Publication Data
Thornton, Kim Campbell.
The "I have a life" dog owner's guide / by Kim Campbell Thornton and Debra Eldredge.
p. cm.
ISBN 1-59337-593-X
1. Dogs. I. Eldredge, Debra. II. Title.
SF427.T492 2006
636.7--dc22

2006013593
This book is available at quantity discounts for bulk purchases. For information, please call 1-800-872-5627.

This publication is designed to provide accurate and authoritative information with regard to the subject matter covered. It is sold with the understanding that the publisher is not engaged in rendering legal, accounting, or other professional advice. If legal advice or other expert assistance is required, the services of a competent professional person should be sought.

—From a *Declaration of Principles* jointly adopted by a Committee of the American Bar Association and a Committee of Publishers and Associations

Many of the designations used by manufacturers and sellers to distinguish their products are claimed as trademarks. Where those designations appear in this book and Adams Media was aware of a trademark claim, the designations have been printed with initial capital letters.

Cover illustration by Chad Jeffery and Jonathan Santarelli.

Contains portions of material adapted and abridged from *The Everything® Dog Health Book* by Kim Campbell Thornton and Debra Eldredge, D.V.M, ©2005, F+W Publications, Inc. and *The Everything® Labrador Retriever Book* by Kim Campbell Thornton, ©2004, F+W Publications, Inc.

Contents

Introduction

IF YOU'VE RECENTLY become a new dog parent—or you're on the verge of making this big decision—you probably don't need this book to tell you it's a task that's equal parts work and fun. Dogs bring us so much love and enjoyment that once we have one, it's hard to imagine life without them. But they also bring huge responsibility. Like kids, dogs need plenty of care, attention, guidance, and affection—and they don't come with built-in instructions. Inevitably, when it comes to raising a dog, there are many moments where you're left scratching your head wondering, "How should I handle this?" or "Why the heck does Rover do that?" Rest assured these are common concerns, and you can learn to field every one of them in time.

Except, if you're like pretty much everyone else these days, you have tons to do, and never enough time to get it all done. Let's get one thing straight up front: Raising, caring for, and training a dog does take a lot of time. To be a really good dog parent, you need to be ready, willing, and able to invest your time and energy—and make some adjustments to your lifestyle. That said, you also don't want to waste too much time fumbling for solutions and wondering how to do things properly. You need the basics—a guide that will bring you up to dog speed as soon as possible, so you can get a handle on things and start out on the right path building a strong relationship with your dog.

That's where *The "I Have a Life" Dog Owner's Guide* comes in. Think of this as your crash course in dog essentials. Maybe you don't have time to read ten different books on everything from dog nutrition and training to first aid and other medical issues. But you can certainly plow through this one, which packs it all into one small volume. Read on, and you'll get an overview of essentials for pups and older dogs, including anatomy, nutrition, grooming, and other basic wellness tips. Then you'll move on to some basic training, such as how to get your dog to go outside as well as key commands, like "Sit," "Come," and "Stay," to help the two of you work well together as a team. And let's not forget that proper socialization is a must—a well-behaved canine needs to learn good manners, too, if he's going to be an enjoyable member of your family. There are also important things you need to know when it comes to caring for your dog's health—like what to do about those pesky parasites, common ailments, and first aid for your furry friend. It's a lot to think about, and it's all in here, in a common-sense, easy-to-use format that won't leave you guessing.

Pay attention to the strategies and tips this book has to offer, and you'll soon be a natural. You'll have everything under control, and Rover won't run rampant because you've taken the time to train, socialize, and care for him properly. You'll establish yourself as a great pack leader, and the two of you can get on with the business of enjoying a long, happy life together.

Part 1

A Dog Owner's Overview

Chapter 1

Puppy Time

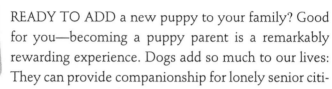 READY TO ADD a new puppy to your family? Good for you—becoming a puppy parent is a remarkably rewarding experience. Dogs add so much to our lives: They can provide companionship for lonely senior citizens, bond as no other best friend can with children, act as a wonderful sounding board for upset teenagers, and bring some much-needed activity to empty nesters' homes. Just like people, dogs are social animals and are happiest when they are included in as many family activities as possible. This makes them wonderful pets. But along with the joys of pup parenting also come huge responsibilities.

The Facts of the Matter

Just like young children, puppies thrive on love, attention, and guidance. They need frequent bathroom breaks, lots of playtime, training to help them learn behavior basics, socialization, and exercise. You should only get a pup if you are willing to put in plenty of effort. Puppies are a major time commitment for the first six months. But even as they get older, don't expect you can slack off. Remember, you're signing up for the long haul! After all, you wouldn't be interested in getting a puppy if you didn't want to spend time together and develop a wonderful bond, right?

Unless your heart is set on a puppy and you are sure you have the time, energy, and proper situation to deal with raising a baby dog, consider adopting an adult dog. Breeders sometimes have young adults who need homes if they aren't going to be show dogs. Rescue groups foster and screen dogs carefully. And there are plenty of wonderful dogs in shelters. Often, these dogs already have some basic training—they don't have accidents in the house, they know how to walk on a leash, and they might even be past the chewing stage. You'll also have the benefit of knowing their full-grown size, temperament, and activity level.

If after careful consideration you still think you want a puppy and you honestly have the time and energy to devote to her, you need to know how to choose the right one.

Finding the Perfect Pup

Okay, just like people, no pup is *totally perfect*. But you can find the pup that's perfect for you. The key to puppy success is choosing the right puppy for your family from the start, so do your research! There are excellent books and Web sites that can help you choose the right puppy for your lifestyle. Talk to your veterinarian and animal shelter staff, and attend a local dog show. Meet lots of puppies and adult dogs of different breeds. While an Old English sheepdog puppy is a cute teddy bear, an adult might be a bit overwhelming for the average family.

Canine Considerations

Before you choose your pup, make a list of priorities for your family and lifestyle. Do you enjoy grooming? Or are you an immaculate housekeeper who doesn't want to deal with dog hair? What about exercise? Is yours an outdoorsy family that likes to hike and camp, or are you homebodies who prefer to spend weekends curled up with a good book? Considering such factors will help you to choose a dog you'll enjoy and who'll be happy living with you!

Doggie Dilemmas: "Can we have a dog—puh-leez?"
Never adopt a dog simply because your kids beg for one. Dogs are fun, but they're a lot of work. No matter how much your kids love their dog, you can't rely on them to do the caretaking and training. Might as well face it—that will be your job. Unless you want a dog and are prepared to do the parenting yourself, you're barking up the wrong tree!

Here's a checklist of things to think about when choosing a dog:

- Size
- Grooming requirements

- Exercise needs
- Special equipment needs (such as a very large crate for a giant-breed dog)
- Ease of training
- Behavior around children
- Temperament (friend to all or a bit of a guard dog?)
- Activities (such as agility or obedience)

Luckily, dogs come in a variety of sizes, coats, colors, and temperaments. No doubt there is a puppy who's just right for you!

A Clean Bill of Health

With so many options, it might seem tough to know which dog to choose. There are some basic health issues to watch for that will make the process easier. First off, a puppy should be clean and in good condition. Some breeds tend to be roly-poly as pups, but being too fat is not good, and a distended belly could be a sign of roundworm infestation. Beware of pups with diarrhea, goopy eyes, lackluster coats, and sneezing or coughing. Avoid puppies with reddened skin and those who seem to scratch excessively. Open sores are a warning that the pup could have skin or immunity problems. The pup's skin should be elastic and snap back into place after you tent it up gently; this shows the puppy is not dehydrated. Look for hernias—out-of-place bulges—usually near the umbilicus (generally a minor problem) or in the groin (a more difficult problem that needs to be fixed surgically).

 The Doggone Truth: Big Paws to Fill
Did you know you can't always judge how big a pup will get by the size of his feet? Some medium-sized dogs like English springer spaniels have large paws, while a Siberian husky has tight, smaller feet.

Pups should be active and energetic. Look for a puppy with a middle-of-the-road attitude—one who comes up to greet you but isn't frantic—and avoid the pup hanging back in the corner alone.

What Does the Breeder Say?

Many breeders will do a puppy temperament test to see which pups might be easier or harder to train, as well as which would do best in particular types of families. While these tests are not infallible, when you combine them with the breeder's own impressions of the litter, they can help you get a true feel for the puppies' personalities.

While all dogs have many of the same care requirements, certain breeds have unique needs. Large-breed puppies need careful diet plans to help their bones develop properly. Toy-breed puppies might need extra nutritional snacks to keep their blood sugar up. Your breeder can tell you these sorts of things and also give you guidelines to see if your pup is growing normally.

puppy time

7

Reputable breeders will ask you as many questions as you ask them. This is a good sign. It shows they put a great deal of thought and love into breeding their dogs and they only want the best possible homes for their pups. Good breeders also feel a responsibility for their pups and will have you sign a contract so that if anything goes wrong, the puppy will come back to them.

Do Some More Investigating

Once you've narrowed it down to a breed or even a particular pup, try to meet both parents. If the father is not local, you should at least get to meet the dam. A mother dog might be cautious, but she should be basically friendly.

 The Doggone Truth: Love at First Sight?

Try not to fall in love with the first puppy you see. Look at several litters, so you'll have a better idea of which puppy will fit best in your family.

You should know what genetic problems can occur in the breed you're interested in. Ask to see certifications that the parents are free of hip dysplasia, elbow problems, and eye problems if those are common in that breed.

If breeders assure you their dogs never have problems so they don't need to do screenings, beware! If it sounds too good to be true, it probably is.

Puppy Chow

So you've found a pup, and now you need to get down to basics—the most immediate being what to feed the little fur ball. A puppy has different nutritional needs than an adult dog. Puppies grow rapidly. Small breeds can reach adult size by six to eight months, while giant breeds can continue to grow for eighteen to twenty-four months. Growing requires extra vitamins and minerals, and these must be present in the correct ratios. Pups need different amounts of protein and energy sources as well. Too much can be as bad as too little!

Puppies need more calories per pound than an adult dog. It is important not to let your pup get overweight, though. Extra weight adds stress to those growing bones and can lead to arthritis problems later in life.

FIDO **The Doggone Truth: Special Food Formulas**

Don't assume that a special diet for large-breed puppies is a marketing gimmick. Regular puppy food provides complete and balanced nutrition for any size dog, but a food formulated for large-breed puppies is fine-tuned to meet their precise growth needs.

Dogs who'll weigh fifty pounds or more at maturity need a special diet to help them grow slowly and not put weight on too quickly, which can cause skeletal problems. Large- and giant-breed dogs require a carefully balanced calcium diet with fewer calories and lower levels of protein to help them mature at a controlled rate.

Your pup's food should say "Balanced and complete for all life stages" or be specifically labeled as "puppy food." The best foods will not only have a complete nutritional analysis on the label but will state somewhere that they were tested with feeding trials. A laboratory analysis is not a substitute for actually testing a diet by feeding it to dogs. Premium dog foods have been thoroughly tested and will fit the bill.

Before you bring your new puppy home, ask about the food she's been eating. Try to use that food at least for the first week or so to make the new home transition easier for your pup. If you intend to switch foods, do so gradually over a week or so.

Feeding Time

Your veterinarian and breeder can help you work out the best diet for your pup. Discuss how much to feed and how often, as well as which foods are best. Remember that the amounts written on dog food bags or cans are simply guidelines. You need to feed your pup as an individual. Most pups do best with three meals a day until four months or so, and then stay on two meals daily from then on.

Doggie Dilemmas: An Overly Plump Pup

Make sure your puppy isn't getting too fat. He should have a clearly defined waistline. If he looks more like a plump little sausage, you might be feeding too much.

Feeding at specific mealtimes is preferable to leaving a bowl of food out for your dog to graze on. With set meals, you know right away if your pup isn't feeling well. You can easily keep track of how much your pup is eating, and it helps with house-training on a schedule. Puppies should always have access to fresh water, except maybe before bedtime or a long car trip, to avoid accidents.

The Truth about Treats

Let's face it—in addition to his regular food, you're going to give your puppy treats and chew items. Treats can help train your pup and develop your close bond. Just remember that if you use a lot of treats in training, you might need to cut back on your pup's mealtime amounts. Most puppies are happy to use their regular food as training treats, but if you want special treats, talk to your veterinarian. Don't forget about things like chopped apples or carrots. These are healthy, low-calorie treats, and they're good for your dog's teeth!

Stock Up on Supplies

You'll need important supplies to help your new pup settle into your home. Here are some essentials.

Crate

This metal or plastic cage will serve as your pup's bedroom. He will sleep in it at first, take naps there, and rest safely while you are busy or away from home. A crate can double as a carrier on car trips or airline flights. It will also help with house-training—puppies don't like to mess in their room, even if they don't mind going on your best rug! Crates are also a great alternative to confining your pup to one small room, because they can be moved around your house. That way your pup can still be involved with the family, even at night or during mealtimes.

Don't feel like it's mean to confine your pup to her crate. Puppies like to have a cozy space to call their own. Many dogs will go into their crates for a rest even as adults with the run of the house. For them it's a safe den—a quiet retreat from guests, too much activity, and other pets.

The crate also keeps your pup safe when you're busy and can't be watching her closely. Otherwise, she could be chewing on poisonous plants, biting into electrical cords, or chomping on dangerous household items.

Collars and Leads

Your pup should have a collar with a buckle, plastic snap, or safety release—not a chain or prong collar. And don't forget identification tags and a rabies tag, once she is vaccinated.

A leather or canvas lead is easier on your hands than a chain or nylon one. Stay away from flexible or retractable leads at first. These are not good for puppies. You don't want your pup to learn to pull on

the leash. It is also easy for people and dogs to get tangled up and hurt
by the thin line.

Canine Quick Fix: Extra ID

Microchips are an additional form of identification inserted under the
skin with a needle. Each tiny chip has a unique number that can be read
with a scanner. This number is linked to information necessary to return
your dog home if she gets lost.

Toys

Make sure any toys you choose are "puppy safe"—filled with non-
toxic stuffing. Breakable plastic is definitely not safe. And watch that
your pup doesn't get a hold of any squeakers she could swallow after
tearing up a toy. With the exception of toys like Kongs and Guma-
bones or Nylabones, which are exceptionally tough, very few toys
should be left with an unsupervised pup.

There's More

You're not done stocking up yet. Your pup will also need:

- **A comfy bed:** Make sure it's soft, fluffy, and easy to wash.
- **Stainless steel bowls for food and water:** These are nonallergenic
  (unlike some plastics), and easy to clean. No pottery bowls until

your pup is older. You don't want her chewing on and breaking them.

- 🐾 **Brushes:** A thin hound cloth works for dogs with short, tight coats, such as greyhounds, but long-coated dogs like collies need a slicker brush and a pin brush.
- 🐾 **Soft cotton balls:** These are a must for ear cleaning.
- 🐾 **Teeth-cleaning supplies:** A child's soft toothbrush works well. Make sure to use dog toothpaste (people toothpaste is meant to be spit out, plus it doesn't come in yummy flavors like poultry).
- 🐾 **Dog towels:** These are essential for quick drying after a romp in the rain.

Is Your Home Puppy Proof?

Keeping your puppy safe from your home—and vice versa—can be a challenge. Supervision is key to prevention, as is keeping your pup out of places where he can cause trouble. Baby gates work wonders, and they don't just block off doorways. They can be used to separate pets, so your cat doesn't feel threatened by this unmannerly newcomer. They'll also keep the pup off your heirloom Oriental rug.

Anything the pup shouldn't have must be kept out of reach. Dangerous household items such as bleach and cleaners should be in locked cupboards. Electrical cords need to be moved or covered with plastic hosing for extra protection. Puppies are notorious burglars. Shoes need to be in closets, and even books should be put where the pup can't easily reach. A large-breed pup will quickly grow big enough to reach the kitchen counters, so check there, too. As for your kids' toys—they'll learn to pick up and put their toys away after the pup chews a few of their things.

Canine Quick Fix: Chew Stoppers

If your puppy thinks furniture legs taste good, there are some things you can try to protect them. Wrap them in aluminum foil; no dog wants to bite down on that. You can also coat wood with Bitter Apple to repel your dog. The paste form often works better than the spray.

Don't forget to protect your doorways. Make sure right from the start that your pup can't barrel past you out into an unfenced yard or the street. This is one more good reason to use gates and to start training the "Wait" command early on.

Get into a Groove

Just like human babies, puppies do best on a routine. This keeps the fussing to a minimum and helps with house-training. Keep in mind that your pup has no sense of the days of the week. If you get up at 6 A.M. on Monday through Friday to give him a short walk and breakfast, don't expect him to sleep in until 8 A.M. on Saturday.

Along with a feeding and walking routine, you need to establish family limits for your pup. Is the pup allowed on furniture? If so, which furniture? Is the pup allowed to sleep on a bed if he behaves properly, or is it best for all if he sleeps on his own soft bed next to yours? The important thing is that everyone consistently sticks with these house rules so the pup doesn't get confused.

Canine Quick Fix: On a Short Leash

If you're concerned about your pup wandering around the house and getting into trouble, but you don't want to crate him all the time, keep him on leash inside the house so he stays at your side. This is a good way for him to learn to look to you for guidance.

The Well-Groomed Pooch

Grooming can be a wonderful time to bond with your pup. Start early, so your dog gets used to these routines.

Brushing

Initially, gently use a soft brush or cloth to rub over your pup's back. If she resists, feed her a treat while you do this. It also helps to talk to your pup in a positive voice—telling her how beautiful she is and how she'll look even more beautiful when you're done. That sounds silly, but dogs truly respond to your voice and the emotions it conveys even if they don't understand every word.

If you have a longhaired pup, try to do a little grooming every day. That way the pup isn't bored, and you stay on top of any tangles or mats. If grooming is too much for you, make regular appointments with a professional groomer. Mats can be quite painful for your dog, and they can cover up skin problems that need attention. Make sure when you brush that you get your pup's entire body. And even short-coated dogs need a wipe with a damp cloth sometimes to pick up loose hair and any dirt buildup.

Nail Trimming

Get your pup used to having his feet handled so nail trimming is not traumatic. (Use treats to help your dog get comfortable with nail trimming.) Be sure to have your veterinarian or breeder demonstrate how to do nails correctly and safely, though. Carefully removing the tips of the nails will not hurt, but cutting too far down will!

Doggie Dilemmas: What an Earful!

Dogs with long, hanging ears, such as spaniels or retrievers, often develop ear infections. The inside of the ears is warm and moist, an ideal home for bacteria to flourish. To prevent problems, keep ears clean and dry, especially if your dog loves to swim.

Cleaning Eyes and Ears

Pups should also be comfortable with you carefully wiping any discharge from their eyes with a damp cloth and checking their ears. This daily routine, followed with a small treat, will make it easier for you and your veterinarian if your dog ever has a problem. When you clean the eyes, check for any redness or squinting that could indicate irritation or injury. Sniff the ears to make sure they don't smell bad. If they do, your puppy might have an ear infection that needs veterinary attention.

Chapter 2

As Your Dog Grows

 SO FOR HOW LONG will you be dealing with a baby pooch, if you have one? Dogs reach physical and emotional maturity when they hit eighteen to twenty-four months. They might *look* fully grown long before then, but they're still developing. It might even seem like your two-and-a-half or three-year-old dog still acts like a pup! It's not unheard of, especially with some particularly active or rambunctious breeds. Be patient with your dog's puppy-like enthusiasm and adolescent testing of your authority. Although some pup parents just don't believe it when they're in the throes of the "terrible twos," canine style, your little devil really will grow up and settle down eventually.

As dogs reach maturity, there are new things to think about. Their nutritional and exercise needs change. If they're longhaired, their coat comes into full glory. And appropriate diet, grooming, dental care, and exercise are all essential to keep your adult dog in peak condition. Here's a quick rundown of these and other details you'll need to stay on top of as your pup grows up.

Grown-Up Nutrition

Your dog's nutritional needs depend in large part on his breed and size. Some dogs reach physical maturity rapidly, while others—particularly large-breed puppies—take longer to mature. Although dogs' growth starts to slow at about six months, large and giant-breed dogs don't reach full physical maturity until they're two and sometimes even three years old. They should eat a large-breed puppy diet or a diet customized by your veterinarian until they're two.

Small dogs of any age, especially those who weigh less than twenty pounds, have a higher metabolic rate than large-breed dogs, so they burn energy more quickly. They need a nutrient-dense diet that gives them a lot of nutrition in a small amount of food. Most small and medium-size dogs can start eating a food formulated for adult dogs at nine months to one year. By then, their skeleton will be full size, or almost there. Small but stocky breeds, such as pugs, are exceptions. They're also prone to skeletal problems if they grow too quickly. They can start eating adult food as early as five months of age.

What's the Right Weight?

What if you don't know how big your puppy is going to be? Mixed-breed puppies adopted from animal shelters don't come with papers detailing their parents' breed or size. Don't sweat it—there's a rule of thumb that will get you in the ballpark. Take the puppy's weight at eight weeks. Multiply by four or five, and the result is an estimate of his adult size. This estimate won't be exact, but it can help you figure out whether you're feeding to fuel the growth of a peanut-sized pooch or a mountain of a dog!

Time to Switch

Whether you're ready to feed your puppy adult food, or you simply want to change brands, always do so gradually. Dogs have sensitive stomachs, and a rapid dietary change can bring on vomiting or diarrhea. Begin by adding small amounts of the new food to your dog's regular food over a period of five to ten days. The more different the foods are from one another (for instance, if you're switching from dry food to canned food or vice versa), the more gradual the change should be. Whatever you choose to feed your dog, be sure that it offers complete and balanced nutrition for his life stage.

Senior Nutrition

A healthy older dog can stick to his usual diet as long as he maintains a good weight and his coat and skin are shipshape. If he starts to pack on some pounds, though, a change in diet might be in order. Like people, dogs tend to become less active with age, so they need fewer calories to maintain an appropriate weight. Because their aging body is less able to metabolize protein efficiently, they need a food with reduced fat and calories, but high levels of protein. Added fiber can also cut calories while still filling your dog's belly.

Older dogs can also develop a thinner coat or dry, itchy skin. Certain nutritional supplements may help, such as essential fatty acids, vitamin E, and zinc. Ask your veterinarian for a recommendation. Checking thyroid levels is important on older dogs with weight gain or coat changes as well.

Grooming, Part 2

Hopefully, if you got your dog used to grooming as a puppy she might even look forward to it as an adult. After all, what's nicer than having someone else brush your hair? Brushing is great for keeping your dog's skin in good condition, and it promotes blood circulation and new hair growth.

A complete canine grooming session involves brushing and combing the coat; checking the skin for signs of itchiness, parasites, or injuries; cleaning the eyes and ears; and taking care of nails. Depending on your dog's coat type, size, and lifestyle, grooming can take as little as five minutes to as much as twenty or more minutes each day.

Canine Quick Fixes: Grooming Tables

If you want to save on back strain, consider a grooming table. This is a good way to keep your dog at eye level, so you don't have to hunch over. Choose one with a grooming arm and noose to hold him in place. If a grooming table isn't an option, you can always groom your dog on top of a picnic table or your washer or dryer.

To manage shedding, most dogs should be brushed daily, especially if you've got a breed who sheds a ton—such as German shepherds, Dalmatians, Labrador retrievers, and pugs. If your shorthaired dog doesn't shed heavily, a weekly brushing is sufficient.

Brushing Your Shorthaired Dog

A rubber curry brush that fits over the hand is a safe bet for most shorthaired dogs. Known as a hound mitt or glove, this brush is covered with nubby bristles. A curry brush should fit comfortably in your hand and might have a strap to help you keep a firm grip when brushing. You can find curry brushes and hound mitts at well-stocked pet-supply stores. Also get a steel comb with wide and narrow teeth to help remove tangles.

Canine Quick Fix: Excess Shedding
If fur is flying off of your pooch every time you touch him, brush him thoroughly and give him a warm bath. Then blow-dry him, brushing as you go, until he's completely dry. This will help loosen and remove excess hair.

Hold the brush firmly, or put on the hound mitt, and rub it over the coat in the direction the fur grows. Brush all the way down to the skin to remove dirt, skin-cell debris, and loose hairs. You might want to brush outside or in the garage, or else brush the dog while he's standing on a sheet so you can get rid of the dirt and hair easily when you're through.

Breeds that shed heavily might also benefit from a shedding blade, shedding comb, or wire slicker brush. These tools have sharp edges or teeth that remove excess coat. Use them once or twice a week, after first brushing with the curry. Move it over the body in the direction the hair grows. Don't bear down too hard, or the sharp edges might injure your dog, and don't use it on the legs or areas where the hair is thin and fine, such as the belly. Avoid using shedding tools too often—you'll remove too much coat!

Brushing Your Longhaired Dog

With longhaired dogs, mats and tangles come with the territory. Daily brushing helps keep these problems under control. You'll need a pin brush, a shedding comb, a wire slicker brush or shedding blade, and a bristle brush. A pin brush, which has long metal "pins" coming out of the pad, helps lift out loose hair and skin debris without removing a lot of undercoat. When you're finished grooming, use the pin brush to fluff the coat by brushing against the direction of the hair. A shedding or dematting comb helps break mats into manageable sections you can comb. You can also use the slicker brush to gently remove knots and tangles. The bristle brush brings out shine once the other tools work their magic. When your dog is "blowing," or shedding coat, a shedding blade comes in handy to remove all that excess hair.

Run the pin brush through the coat in the direction of the hair. Check for mats behind the ears, on the backs of the legs, in the groin area, and on the tail. If necessary, use the shedding comb to remove mats. Work at it slowly, starting at the bottom of the mat and working toward the skin, being careful not to pull. Avoid cutting the mat; that will only make the area more prone to matting. Spend just a few minutes each day removing tangles before they get bad, and you'll save time in the long run. You'll also save your dog pain.

What to Do with Wirehaired Dogs

Besides the usual brushes and combs, to groom a wirehaired dog you'll need trimming and thinning scissors, a stripping knife or two, and a set of clippers. You can keep a wire coat in good condition with weekly brushing. Use a pin brush or a natural bristle brush. First brush in the opposite direction the hair grows, then brush with the direction. Care for leg and facial hair with a wire slicker brush. The slicker brush is also good for removing undercoat.

as your dog grows

To maintain its correct hard texture, a wire coat must also be stripped twice a year. No, that doesn't mean taking your dog in for a wax job. Stripping removes dead hair and shapes the coat. You can strip the coat by hand or with a special tool called a stripping knife. Your breeder or a dog groomer can show you how to do this and advise you on which stripping knives and scissors to purchase. If stripping seems like too much work, you can simply have the coat clipped. Just know that this will soften the texture and color of the hair. If you want your dog to maintain the proper wire look, stripping is the way to go.

Wirehaired breeds' eyebrows and beard must be trimmed and shaped. Before you start, wash the furnishings (as facial hair is known) and work in some cornstarch or grooming chalk. Comb the hair forward and use scissors to trim. If you plan to show your dog, ask your breeder or another experienced person for advice on how to get the proper look.

 FIDO **The Doggone Truth: Dogs and Sunburn**

All dogs can get sunburned, not just hairless breeds. If your dog spends lots of time in the sun, apply sunscreen to his nose, ears, belly, and any other areas that aren't well protected by hair. Use sunscreen that's safe if your dog licks it off—pet supply stores and veterinarians carry canine sunscreen.

Get in the Bath Tub!

There are two truths about giving a dog a bath: One, it's easier if you're organized; and two, even if you're organized, you'll still get wet. Gather everything you'll need before you even think about running water and calling your dog. That includes:

- ❧ Two or three towels
- ❧ A washcloth for cleaning the face
- ❧ Cotton balls for inside the ears
- ❧ Mineral oil to protect eyes from soapy water
- ❧ Dog shampoo and conditioner
- ❧ A hair dryer
- ❧ A rubber mat for the tub floor to keep you both on sure footing

A large walk-in shower with a seat and a handheld nozzle is ideal for your small or medium-size dog. You can also bathe small dogs (up to about twenty pounds) in the kitchen sink, which is easier on your back than bending over a tub.

Suds Up

Before you start scrubbing, brush your dog thoroughly to work out mats or tangles. If they get wet, they'll tighten up and it will be even tougher to remove them. Using warm water, wet your dog down to the skin, starting at the head and working your way back. Apply shampoo,

27

again starting at the head. Massage it in thoroughly. Rinse with warm water until no more suds are running out of the coat. Shampoo residue can make a dog's coat look dull and flaky, so rinse thoroughly. Apply conditioner if you use it, and rinse again.

Grab a towel and start drying your dog. Stop for a minute, and he'll shake, splattering water everywhere. If you have a longhaired dog, squeeze the water out of the hair on the ears, legs, and tail. By now your first towel will probably be pretty wet, so grab another one and dry your dog some more before you let him out of the shower or tub.

Doggie Dilemmas: The Bath Time Summons

Unless your dog loves bath time, never call her to come for a bath (or anything else unpleasant, such as getting medication). She'll quickly get the idea that coming when you call is a bad idea. Instead, go and get her. That way, she won't associate the "Come" command with doing something she doesn't like.

Drying Time

It's easiest to blow-dry your dog's coat on a surface that puts him at eye level, like a grooming or picnic table. If you have a dog who's small enough to hold in your lap, that might be an option too. Whatever the case, just be sure your dog can't get away, or else you'll be chasing a wet dog all over the house.

Set the dryer on warm, not hot. Hold it several inches away from your dog's body, and keep it moving so you don't accidentally burn her skin. Brush through the coat as you dry to remove more loose hair, using a curry for shorthaired dogs and a pin brush for longhaired dogs. It's fine if you let your dog air-dry partway in her crate; just be sure she's not catching a draft.

When you finally turn her loose, she'll probably go running through the house, rolling on the carpet to get rid of that funny shampoo/conditioner smell. Be warned: If you let her outdoors right after a bath, she'll roll in the first dirty thing she can find!

Keep Those Chompers Clean

People are always complaining about bad doggie breath. Not surprisingly, periodontal disease is one of the most common problems veterinarians see in dogs. Brushing your dog's teeth daily—or at least several times a week—will help prevent buildup of bacteria-trapping plaque, which hardens into ugly brown tartar and eventually causes gum disease. Your dog's breath will smell much better, and he'll keep more of his teeth as he ages. He'll have fewer bacteria circulating in his system, and he'll also need fewer expensive veterinary cleanings.

Brushing Your Dog's Teeth

Use a toothbrush and toothpaste made especially for dogs. The toothbrush should have a long handle, soft bristles, and an angled head for ease of brushing. Some dog toothbrushes have two ends, one large for cleaning the front teeth and one small for cleaning the teeth way in the back of the mouth. You can also use a small, nubby rubber brush that fits over your finger like a thimble. This can be the best choice for puppies or small dogs. Doggie toothpaste should contain enzymes to fight plaque. Some varieties have fluoride to help control bacteria. Avoid using toothpaste made for people, which can contain baking soda, detergents, or salts that can upset your dog's stomach. Many dog toothpastes are flavored like beef or chicken to add to their appeal.

Canine Quick Fix: Chew Right

If your puppy enjoys chewing, encourage him to chew on the right things. Chewing helps keep the teeth clean. Chew toys that assist in dental care, such as enzymatic chew sticks and ridged Kong chews, are great options.

If your dog didn't get used to tooth-brushing as a puppy, work up to it by wiping out his mouth daily with a damp washcloth or piece of gauze. After a couple of weeks, he'll be used to having you touch his mouth and teeth, and you can introduce the brush and toothpaste.

Starting where the teeth and gums meet, hold the brush at a 45-degree angle and gently move in an oval pattern. Be sure to get the bristles between the teeth as well as at the base of the tooth. The upper teeth in the back are most important, but try to get all teeth if possible.

Cleanings at the Vet

When yellow or brown plaque has built up on your dog's teeth, he needs more than home tooth brushing. A veterinary cleaning, done under anesthesia, has three purposes: to immobilize your dog for a thorough cleaning; to prevent him from feeling any pain during the cleaning; and to allow the veterinarian to place a tube into the wind-pipe, which prevents bacteria from entering the respiratory system.

Doggie Dilemmas: Is Anesthesia Safe?

Today, veterinary anesthetics are very safe. Preanesthetic blood work can help to plan the safest anesthetic procedures for dogs with health risks. A good veterinarian will also have equipment to monitor your dog during the cleaning to provide even greater safety.

Before a professional cleaning, the veterinarian will give your dog a physical exam. He might order preanesthetic blood work, depending on your dog's age and condition. Once your dog is anesthetized, the veterinarian will thoroughly examine his mouth, remove tartar, scale the area below the gum line, polish the teeth, rinse the mouth, and apply fluoride. Afterward, he may prescribe antibiotics to ward off potential bacterial infections.

Get Your Dog Moving

From the tiniest toy breeds all the way up to the giants of the canine world, all dogs need exercise and play to keep them healthy and mentally sharp. A dog who lies around all the time will get dull and depressed. Dogs are active animals, and they need interaction with people and other dogs. Daily walks, indoor and outdoor play, and training sessions will keep your dog in good physical health and boost mental well-being.

The amount of exercise your dog needs depends on her age, breed, and individual activity level. In any case, your goal is to keep your dog from becoming soft and flabby!

All puppies need lots of free play—running loose in an enclosed yard, chasing balls, and so on. This helps build strong muscles and bones. Puppies also need to practice walking nicely on leash. Protect puppies from jumping on and off furniture and running on hard surfaces, both of which can injure their growing bones and joints.

Sporting, working, terrier, and herding breeds are often the most active. Be ready to give them at least thirty minutes to an hour of good, hard exercise every day. Jogging and dog sports like agility and flyball are great ways to give these dogs the action they crave.

Chapter 3

A Quick Anatomy Lesson

 YOU'VE GOT TONS to learn about canine health and well-being if you want to be a good dog parent, and you'll need to know a bit about anatomy for that. Don't worry—you don't need a load of college courses to get familiar with your dog's anatomy. This chapter will highlight anatomy basics essential to understanding how your dog's body works so you'll be able to take better care of her. What follows is a guide to your dog's skin, fur, bones, joints, musculature, mouth, eyes, and ears.

The Look of Things

Dogs may well be the most genetically diverse species on earth. How many other species can claim such a range in size, appearance, and coat type? No matter what the breed or mix, though, all dogs share some common external features.

Here are some key anatomical terms:

- 🐾 **Stop:** The indentation between the eyes where the nasal bones and skull meet (where the muzzle rises up to become the skull)

- 🐾 **Muzzle:** The area in front of the eyes, consisting of the nasal bones, nostrils, and jaws
- 🐾 **Ear leather:** The flap of the ear
- 🐾 **Flews:** The hanging part of a dog's upper lip
- 🐾 **Carpus:** The area where the front leg joins the paw (corresponds to the human wrist)
- 🐾 **Crest:** The upper arched part of the neck
- 🐾 **Withers:** The high point at the top of the shoulders from which a dog's height is measured
- 🐾 **Brisket:** The lower part of the chest; also known as the breastbone or the sternum
- 🐾 **Stifle:** The knee
- 🐾 **Loin:** The area between the ribs and the hip bone

Skin Deep

Just as with humans, the skin contains your dog's body. It protects internal organs, bones, and joints from injury and keeps out harmful organisms. Although it does serve as protection, canine skin is thin, sensitive, and more susceptible to damage than human skin. That's one of the reasons why dogs have a protective covering of fur. Skin is made up of three layers: the epidermis, the dermis, and the subcutis.

The epidermis is the outer layer, beneath the fur. Some parts of the epidermis are delicate and sensitive, such as the groin (the area where the legs meet the body). Tougher, thicker sections of epidermis cover the nose and paw pads. The epidermis contains cells that produce keratin, a protein that's a major component of skin, hair, and toenails; melanin, which gives skin its color; and cells that help the skin generate immune responses.

The dermis is the middle and thickest layer of skin. It consists mainly of collagen fibers, with some elastic fibers to keep skin supple. In the dermis there are mast cells, which help control inflammation. The dermis also contains epidermal appendages: hair follicles, which produce hair; sebaceous glands, which secrete sebum, an oily substance that helps lubricate the skin and coat; and sweat glands. Dogs have two types of sweat glands. The apocrine sweat glands, found throughout the body, produce a scented fluid that may play a role in sexual attraction. The eccrine sweat glands, located in the paw pads and the nasal pad, help dogs regulate their body temperature.

The subcutis, also known as the hypodermis, supports the dermis and the epidermis. It's made up of fat cells and connective tissue, through which nerves and blood vessels supply the skin.

Facts on Fur

Dogs come in a variety of coat types, from the long, silky coat of the Afghan hound or papillon, to the short, thick coat of the pointer or Great Dane, or the curly or wavy coat of the Portuguese water dog and American water spaniel. The reason for this plethora of canine coats is because different breeds produce different sizes and numbers of primary and secondary hairs.

Where the Hair Comes From

No matter how different the various types might appear, all hair is produced by hair follicles, living cells that lie beneath the skin. Formed by proteins, hair originates in a part of the follicle called the hair bulb and passes through the follicular sheath to emerge at the surface of the skin. Each individual hair is called a hair shaft. Although follicles are living cells, hair itself is a dead structure.

Each follicle produces bundles of seven to fifteen hairs. These bundles usually consist of one long, stiff primary, or guard, hair and a number of finer secondary hairs, which are also called underhairs.

The Doggone Truth: Why Some Dogs Shed Less Than Others
Ever wonder why certain dogs, like poodles and bichon frises, don't seem to shed? Their hair has a longer growth cycle than that of other breeds, so hair isn't replenished as often. If you're a lousy housekeeper, you can go about a month without vacuuming before you start to see poodle dust bunnies.

Different breeds of dogs have different numbers of hairs. The density of hairs per square inch varies from breed to breed. Don't be fooled if your dog doesn't seem to shed. All dogs shed hair; it's just more apparent with longhaired dogs or dogs with thick undercoats. Paradoxically, dogs with short hair shed the most.

How Dogs' Hair Grows

The life cycle of hair involves growth, rest, loss, and replacement—a process that's called shedding, or blowing coat. Hairs in different parts of the body grow to genetically determined lengths. This is known as the anagen phase of hair growth. Once hair reaches its predetermined length, it rests—the telogen phase. After this rest period, new hair begins forming. As these new hairs rise through the follicular sheath, they push out the old hair, and that's when it lands on your clothes, floor, and furniture.

You've probably noticed that dogs seem to shed more at certain times of the year. That's because hair growth and loss is affected by the number of hours of daylight to which it's exposed. Hair grows thick in the fall, in preparation for cold winter months. As the days grow warmer and longer, all that excess hair falls out, replaced with a cooler summer coat. If your dog spends most of his time indoors, his coat won't be affected as much by these seasonal cycles, and he will probably shed small amounts year-round.

Hormones also affect shedding. Unspayed females usually shed twice a year, at the same time they're in heat. Spayed females, on the other hand, usually develop a very full coat because they don't have that periodic surge of hormones. They're more likely to shed year-round.

How Much Shedding Is Normal?

The first time you see the shed of an Alaskan malamute, chow chow, or other breed with a heavy double coat, you might think the dog has an awful skin disease. The fur comes out in big clumps, and the coat can look pretty patchy and ratty. Don't worry! Unless the dog has actual bald spots, this is normal.

On the other hand, hormonal diseases such as hypothyroidism, certain hereditary abnormalities, and even stress can cause dogs to shed abnormally. Dogs with hypothyroidism often develop symmetrical hair loss on the body. The coat doesn't look healthy, either. It becomes thin or sparse and falls out easily. Dogs whose bodies produce too much cortisone (Cushing's disease) also tend to have this symmetrical hair loss. When stress is a factor, hair loss often occurs in specific areas, such as the rear end, where hair typically grows quickly.

Muscles, Tendons, and Ligaments

Beneath the skin, muscles are body tissues made up of long fibers that contract when they're stimulated, producing motion. The muscles are connected to bones with fibrous tissues called tendons. Ligaments are dense, stiff, stable bands of fibrous tissues that attach one bone to another. Ligaments limit range of motion, which is why your dog's front leg, for instance, bends backward but not upward.

Your dog's body has three types of muscles. Skeletal muscle plays a role in movement; smooth muscle enables the contractions of hollow organs such as blood vessels, the gastrointestinal tract, the bladder, and the uterus; and cardiac muscle ensures the heart keeps beating. Skeletal muscles are the only ones your dog can actually control. The nervous system calls the shots for smooth and cardiac muscles.

Dogs have five muscle groups:

- 🐾 Head and neck muscles
- 🐾 Dorsal (back) muscles
- 🐾 Thoracic, abdominal, and tail muscles
- 🐾 Forelimb muscles
- 🐾 Hind-limb muscles

Muscle Injuries

If you ever notice your dog limping, he might have a muscle sprain or strain, or a tendon injury. Frequently, when canine "weekend warriors" who aren't well conditioned have a round of strenuous exercise—a long walk, an intense Frisbee session, or an obstacle-filled hike, these injuries happen.

Sprains are partial or complete tearing of a muscle or ligament. Torn knee ligaments are especially common. Sprains often happen when a dog slips or slides on a hard, slick surface or falls off furniture. Once a dog has had a sprain, it's likely to recur, so keeping your dog in good condition is important. Recurring sprains can cause joints to become unstable and might lead to arthritis.

FIDO The Doggone Truth: Take Sprains Seriously

Don't treat a sprain lightly—sprains can be more difficult to heal than fractures. Signs of a sprain include tenderness, swelling, bruising, and lameness. X-rays can rule out a fracture and help evaluate the injury.

If your dog has a sprain, lots of rest is a must. The easiest way to do that is to confine your dog to his crate or to a small room such as a bathroom or laundry room. Apply cold packs to the injured area for the first twenty-four hours to help reduce swelling. Use a gauze wrap to attach a chemical cold pack or a bag of frozen peas to the affected area, leaving it for fifteen to thirty minutes. Do this three or four times during the day. On the second and third days, apply warm—not hot—compresses to the area on a similar schedule.

Your veterinarian might prescribe pain relievers (nonsteroidal anti-inflammatory drugs), but these can have the negative effect of causing your dog to use the limb before the injury has healed. Continue to rest him, and take him out to potty on leash to prevent him from running or jumping. It can take as little as three weeks or as long as several months for a sprain to heal, which happens when the body replaces the torn portion of the ligament with new fibrous connective tissue.

Tendon injuries usually occur when a dog suddenly wrenches or twists a limb. Tendons can also become inflamed (tendonitis) after extensive running or other overuse of the leg. The most common tendon injury in dogs is a ruptured Achilles tendon, which needs surgical repair. This often happens to canine athletes such as racing greyhounds, hunting dogs, or agility competitors. Otherwise, most tendon injuries have similar signs as sprains and they require the same treatment.

The Bare Bones Facts

The skeleton is the frame that supports and protects muscles and other soft tissues. It also stores minerals the body needs, such as calcium. The leg and pelvis bones contain bone marrow, which produces red and white blood cells. Bone is a living, renewable component of the body that contains blood vessels and nerves. It's covered with a thin sheath of sensitive tissue, the periosteum, which plays a role in bone growth, repair, and protection.

Joints are the areas where two bones meet. Your dog's major joints are the knees, hips, and elbows. Joints are cushioned by cartilage, a specialized type of connective tissue.

The skeletal system has two major parts:

- 🐾 **The appendicular skeleton:** the leg and pelvis bones (the long bones)
- 🐾 **The axial skeleton:** skull, vertebrae, ribs, and sternum

The long bones have growth plates that produce cartilage, which is converted to bone as the dog grows. At puberty, this bone growth slows, and the growth plates close when the dog reaches physical maturity.

Skeletal Disorders

Dogs are prone to diseases that affect the skeletal system, resulting in lameness or bone deformities. Here are the various types of skeletal diseases:

- 🐾 **Congenital:** a disease a dog is born with.
- 🐾 **Hereditary:** a condition passed on from one or both parents.
- 🐾 **Infectious or inflammatory:** diseases caused by injury, degeneration from age, or bacterial contamination of a joint through a wound
- 🐾 **Metabolic:** diseases that result from too much or too little of a particular hormone or other substance in the body.
- 🐾 **Traumatic:** including injuries such as getting hit by a car and breaking a leg.
- 🐾 **Neoplastic:** diseases caused by cancer

The most common skeletal disorders are hip dysplasia, intervertebral disc disease, patellar luxation (all hereditary), and arthritis (inflammatory).

Hip dysplasia occurs when the head of the hip bone doesn't fit properly into the hip socket. The resulting joint looseness causes inflammation, pain, and lameness. Intervertebral disc disease (IVDD), happens when a ruptured disc puts pressure on the spinal cord or a nerve root. Some skeletal disorders, such as patellar luxation (dislocation of the knee), are easily diagnosed by observing the dog's hoppity gait and range of motion. Others require X-rays or other diagnostic tests. Sometimes they can be corrected surgically, but often rest and pain relief are the only treatments available, especially for such conditions as arthritis.

Doggie Dilemmas: Reducing the Risk of Bone Disease

How can you help reduce the risk of your dog developing a skeletal disorder? Get your puppy from a reputable breeder who makes sure all breeding stock tests clear of skeletal problems. Also, don't overfeed your puppy or adult dog, and prevent him from jumping or running on hard surfaces before his growth plates close.

Open Wide

Your dog's mouth is much like your own. Dogs have lips and cheeks, a slurpy tongue, four pairs of salivary glands, a larynx and pharynx, and an epiglottis. And let's not forget the teeth. Puppies are born toothless. The twenty-eight baby (deciduous) teeth start erupting when they're two or three weeks old. Puppies start losing their baby teeth at about three months and usually have all their adult teeth by four to seven months of age.

Adult dogs have forty-two teeth: twelve incisors, four canines, sixteen premolars, and ten molars. Small dogs often have dental problems because all forty-two teeth are crammed into such a tiny mouth. And some short-faced breeds, such as pugs or bulldogs, might have fewer teeth because there's no room in their mouth for the last molars. Some breeds, such as Doberman pinschers, carry a mutation for missing teeth, and some spaniels and hounds develop extra teeth. These extra teeth should be pulled so they don't crowd, twist, or overlap the normal teeth.

 FIDO **The Doggone Truth: Tongues Wagging**

Eight pairs of muscles and five pairs of nerves control tongue movements. The bumpy projections on the surface of the tongue are called papillae. Black spots on the tongue are common and don't have any medical or other significance. The tongue plays a role in cooling the dog's body (panting). When dogs pant, the saliva on the surface of the tongue evaporates, providing a cooling effect.

Mouth Troubles

The most common mouth problems in dogs are gum inflammation (gingivitis) and periodontal disease, an inflammation of the deeper tooth structures. Other problems include incorrect bites (malocclusions), a hereditary swollen jaw (craniomandibular osteopathy), and inflamed or infected lip folds (lip-fold pyodermas). Mouth injuries range from foreign bodies lodged in the mouth or throat to infections from quills or splinters stuck in the mouth to electrical or chemical burns. Abscessed or broken teeth are also common.

Gingivitis and periodontal disease are preventable with regular tooth brushing and veterinary cleanings as needed. Dogs who have an overshot jaw (the upper jaw protrudes beyond the lower jaw) or an undershot jaw (the lower jaw protrudes beyond the upper jaw) might need orthodontic treatment if the teeth become crowded or displaced. In most cases, however, no treatment is necessary.

Craniomandibular osteopathy, or CMO, is a painful inherited condition that's seen in certain terriers, as well as some other breeds. It usually develops in puppies at four to ten months of age and results from excess bone deposits along the underside of the jaw and on other parts of the jaw and skull. Puppies with CMO usually run a fever, drool, and have little appetite. Aspirin in amounts prescribed by your veterinarian can help control the pain, and the condition sometimes improves with maturity, although complete recovery is rare.

Mouth cancers are rare in dogs, but they can occur. They include melanomas, squamous cell carcinomas, granular cell tumors, and mast cell tumors. They are treatable if caught in time, but can require surgery and radiation.

Managing That Mouth

To keep your dog's mouth healthy, examine it weekly for signs of injury or illness. Watch for raised or bumpy tissue, sores, broken teeth, and bruises or bleeding from the tongue, gums, or roof of the mouth. Look under the tongue to make sure nothing is wedged beneath it. And, of course, check your dog's mouth any time he's drooling or pawing at his mouth or throat.

Doggie Dilemmas: Steer Clear of Sticks

Your dog probably loves chewing on sticks, but they're not good for him. Splinters can get stuck in his mouth or tongue, causing an infection. Buy him regular chew toys instead.

Seeing Clearly

Seeing clearly is complicated business, but the eye is geared up for the challenge. Housed in a socket called the bony orbit, and protected by the upper and lower eyelids as well as the third eyelid (called the haw or sometimes the nictitating membrane), the eyeball is a delicate yet powerful sense organ. The eye is made up of three layers. The fibrous outer layer of connective tissue contains the cornea (which bends incoming light rays and focuses them onto the retina) and the white of the eye, called the sclera. A middle layer called the uvea contains blood vessels and nerves as well as the light-regulating iris and a muscle called the ciliary body, behind the iris. The iris controls the amount of light that enters the eye by adjusting the size of the pupil, the opening in its center. The iris also gives your dog's eyes their color. The inner layer of the eye holds the light-sensitive layer of cells known as the retina, which contains specialized light receptors known as rods and cones. Their job is to convert incoming light into nerve impulses, which are then relayed via the optic nerve to the brain to be processed into an image. Amazingly, all of this occurs in a split second.

A Dog's Sense of Sight

Although dogs tend to have sharper senses than humans, they have relatively poor eyesight. Because dogs evolved as hunters, their eyes are located in the front of their head, which allows them to focus on their prey. This eye placement is good for coordination and accuracy, but it's not so good for peripheral vision. A dog's eye anatomy makes him good at detecting and following movement, as well as seeing in poor light, but he's not so good at recognizing details or differentiating colors. Dogs can see color, but not to the same extent as humans.

Eye Diseases

Eye problems can result from anatomical anomalies (such as too many eyelashes), irritation or injury, infections, or congenital or hereditary conditions. Common signs of eye problems are pain, discharge, redness, and filminess or cloudiness of the eye.

Common eye problems include extra eyelashes, which irritate the eye; eyelid defects such as entropion or ectropion; cherry eye, a congenital defect in which a tear gland bulges out from beneath the eyelid; conjunctivitis, or pink eye; dry eye; corneal injuries; cataracts; glaucoma; and retinal diseases. Depending on the condition, medication or surgery might be in order. Unfortunately, some eye diseases, such as progressive retinal atrophy, have no treatment and lead to eventual blindness. On the up side, dogs can get around well without sight by making more use of their smell and hearing.

Canine Quick Fix: Spotting Eye Trouble

There are ways to tell if your dog's eyes are hurting him. You might notice the eye tearing more than usual or your dog squinting or becoming sensitive to light. He might paw at his eye or whine. The eye might also look red or irritated. Take your dog to the veterinarian if his eye appears to be painful.

All Ears

A dog has an acute sense of hearing, thanks to the structure of his ears. Dogs' ears come in all sorts of shapes and sizes. A dog's ears can be pricked in the air or folded over like the dog-eared page of a book. They might be large or small, long or short. But on the inside, every dog's ear is an acoustic masterpiece.

Ear Anatomy

Sound is energy, or vibration, transmitted by waves through the air. Ever noticed that your dog can wiggle his ears much more than you can? He can also rotate his ear flap (known as the pinna) to capture sounds, which then travel into the ear canal. From there the sound flows through the ear canal downward and inward until it arrives at the eardrum, or tympanic membrane. A chain of small bones called the auditory ossicles then transmits the sound to the inner ear, which resembles a series of bony canals. The inner ear is the essential organ of hearing and contains the cochlea. Coiled like a snail shell, the cochlea is filled with fluid that converts the vibrations making up sound into waves that become nerve impulses transported to the auditory nerve where the brain interprets them. As with sight, all of this occurs instantly.

Ear Troubles

No doubt, dogs' ears are a sore spot. Veterinarians spend as much as 20 percent of their time treating ear infections and other ear problems. Ears can become infected with bacteria, fungi, or yeast. They get injured in fights or play, and they can become infested with mites. Allergies can cause other ear problems on top of all that, and dogs can suffer congenital or acquired deafness, too.

If your dog frequently shakes his head and paws at his ears, he might have an infection and antibiotics could be in order. Your veterinarian will need to culture the buildup in the ear to determine what's causing the infection. This allows her to prescribe the best antibiotic for the job. In the case of itching and inflammation caused by allergies, it's time to call in the big guns: antihistamines and corticosteroids.

If your dog's earflap is wounded, you'll need to stop the bleeding and apply antibiotic ointment to the injured area. A serious laceration might need stitches. Bite wounds often become abscessed, so keep an eye on the area to make sure it doesn't become swollen and tender.

 The Doggone Truth: Now Hear This!

Except for the external ear, dogs and humans have similar ear anatomy, but dogs can hear high-pitched sounds that are inaudible to humans. They can also hear sounds from a much greater distance than people.

With good care, many ear problems can be avoided. Keep your dog's ears clean and dry. Wipe them out with a cotton ball after your dog has a bath or goes swimming. Clean the ears whenever you see a buildup of wax or dirt. Use an ear cleaner your veterinarian recommends, and avoid products that contain alcohol, which stings.

Check the ears frequently to make sure nothing is stuck inside them. Dogs can get grass seeds or other objects caught inside their ears. If they're not removed, an infection can begin. Be careful not to push the object further into the ear. If necessary, take the dog to your veterinarian to have the object removed.

Chapter 4

Feeding Your Dog

 DOGS ARE LITTLE scavengers at heart. In fact, some experts theorize that dogs' propensity for raiding human garbage sites might have played a role in canine domestication. As dogs learned they could score some easy meals off humans, and humans learned they could count on dogs to ward off predators or sound the alarm, the two became fast friends. Now, of course, our dogs depend on us entirely for their meals, and we know a lot more about the best ways to feed them.

Food Facts

Dogs are omnivores. That means they can survive by eating a variety of foods. (Cats, on the other hand, are obligate carnivores, which means they must have meat in their diet.) A balanced diet for dogs contains all the essential nutrients their bodies need to function, in the correct quantities and proportions. Plenty of research has been done on canine nutritional requirements over the past few decades, so rest assured that dogs are eating pretty healthy these days!

The Right Recommendations

When formulating foods, dog-food manufacturers rely on nutrient profiles from the Association of American Feed Control Officials (AAFCO), which are based on commonly used ingredients. These provide recommendations for practical minimum and maximum levels of nutrients in dog foods. The NRC recommendations come from studies in which higher-quality nutrients are used. Without input from the AAFCO, pet foods might be nutritionally deficient.

When you look on a bag or can of dog food, the label should include a statement that the food is formulated to meet the nutritional levels established by AAFCO, or that feeding tests using AAFCO procedures demonstrate the food provides complete and balanced nutrition. Ideally, the manufacturer uses feeding trials to prove that a food is complete and balanced. The 2003 National Research Council (NRC) recommendations contain new information about canine nutritional needs, so it's possible that AAFCO nutrient profiles will change in the near future.

What's in That Food?

Dog-food ingredients must be "generally recognized as safe" (GRAS for short), and dog foods must have labels listing all the ingredients. An ingredient list is good for telling you what's in a food, but it can't tell you the quality of the ingredients. No worries—there are some tricks to reading a label that will help you be a more informed dog-food shopper.

The Doggone Truth: Essential Protein

Dietary protein contains ten essential amino acids that dogs cannot make on their own. The best dog foods have meat protein as the first ingredient, which is higher in quality than protein from grains. Forms of meat protein include meat by-products and meat meals.

While some dog foods might list meat as the first ingredient, if you look farther down the label you might notice that it also lists a particular grain in several different forms, such as wheat flour, flakes, middlings, or bran. Individually, each form of wheat might make up only a small part of the food, but together they may outweigh the meat it contains. Look for a food that contains a balance of meat and grain proteins.

Fine-Tuning Fido's Feeding Schedule

Dogs do best when they eat regular meals at specific times every day because they're less likely to overeat. Consistent mealtimes also help with potty training. Physiologically, dogs have the urge to go after they eat, so by scheduling meals and taking your dog out immediately afterward, you can accustom him to eliminating at certain times. And remember, dogs are creatures of habit. They like knowing that meals will appear at certain times every day.

Time to Eat!

Adult dogs do well on two meals a day, morning and evening. Puppies typically eat three or four meals a day. They're growing, so they need more nutrients than adult dogs. If you aren't able to provide mid-day meals, don't worry. Simply divide the amount of food the puppy needs for the day into two meals, and he'll do just fine. The exception might be a small toy-breed puppy. These little dogs sometimes need a snack between meals to keep their energy levels up. You can do this for any dog by filling a treat ball or cube with kibble.

Proper Eating Habits

By helping your dog develop good eating habits, you can avoid problems with obesity and teach manners at the same time. The first good habit is up to you: Measure your dog's food. Don't just load up the bowl until it's full. Use a measuring cup or a kitchen scale so you feed an appropriate amount. If you're using a measuring cup, give a level cup instead of a heaping one.

Unless your dog is really low to the ground, it's a good idea to use raised feeding dishes. This way, your dog is less likely to slosh water or drop food on the floor. He's also less likely to develop intestinal gas. When dogs have to bend down to swallow their food, they swallow air with it, which later becomes stinky intestinal gas. Raised dishes are also recommended for deep-chested dogs who are prone to bloat, or gastric dilatation volvulus. Dogs who have megaesophagus (a large, flaccid esophagus) also do well with raised feeding dishes, which make it easier for food to move from the esophagus to the stomach.

Canine Quick Fix: Slow Down!

If your dog "inhales" his food, spread it out on a flat surface such as a cookie sheet (use one with raised edges to keep the food inside it). This forces him to slow down and eat at a more reasonable pace.

Teach your dog to wait politely while you prepare his food. Dogs love mealtime, and they'll whirl around in circles or jump up on you while you fix their food to show their appreciation. Channel this energy by asking your dog to sit as you're getting the food. Put the bowl down, tell him to stay, and then give him permission to eat by saying, "Okay!" or "Chow!" This is a great chance for Rex to practice his manners and get an immediate reward.

Dog Foods You Can Buy

For ages, dogs ate whatever scraps people gave them. Then James Spratt developed the first commercial dog food, in the form of a biscuit, a little over 140 years ago. Today, dog owners can choose from a wide variety of commercial canned, dry, frozen, and dehydrated dog foods. Different dogs do better on different types of foods, so which type you choose depends a lot on your individual dog's needs.

Dogs like the taste of canned food, and it has a long shelf life until it's opened. On the down side, canned food is expensive, and it must be refrigerated after it's opened. Dry food is easy to scoop out, measure, and serve. It's less expensive than canned food and doesn't need to be refrigerated, even after it's opened. And dogs often like the crunchy texture. Dry food doesn't have much of a down side, although most dogs, if given a choice, will prefer canned food. You can also go with a happy medium—mixing some canned food with dry food.

More recently, manufacturers have begun preparing frozen and dehydrated foods for dogs. These foods are prepared fresh, made into rolls, cubes, or loaves, and flash frozen so they don't need artificial preservatives. The lack of heat processing preserves heat-sensitive vitamins and amino acids that would otherwise be damaged. The disadvantage is that you have to remember to thaw it before use (although many dogs are satisfied to just gulp it down frozen).

Dehydrated foods (which have all the water removed from them) are prepared at a temperature low enough to preserve the value of the vitamins, minerals, and other nutrients yet high enough to kill any bacteria. Just mix them with warm water, and they're ready to feed. Dehydrated foods have a long shelf life, and they're easy to store. Rehydrated food must be refrigerated if your dog doesn't eat all of it at one sitting, but it's easy to prepare just enough to avoid leftovers.

Types of Dog Foods

Dog food is often categorized as popular, premium, or generic. Popular foods are the national or regional brands that you find in grocery stores. They're made by well-known manufacturers that spend a lot of money researching canine nutritional needs and testing their foods by feeding them to dogs. However, these food formulas can vary from batch to batch, depending on the cost and availability of ingredients. So if your dog has tummy troubles when her diet changes, this is something to think about when choosing dog food. In general, popular foods aren't as digestible as premium foods, but they're of better quality than generic foods.

Premium foods are found primarily in pet supply stores. They contain high-quality ingredients and are prepared according to fixed formulas, meaning the ingredients don't change. Some premium foods might contain organic or human-grade ingredients. Premium foods are expensive, but because of their higher digestibility you can feed less of a premium food than of a popular or generic food, which brings down the cost per serving.

Premium foods are often labeled as organic or natural. The term "natural" doesn't have an official definition. It usually means a food doesn't have any artificial flavors, colors, or preservatives. The term "organic" simply refers to the way plants were grown or animals were raised (usually without the use of pesticides or fertilizers or only certain types of pesticides or fertilizers).

Currently, the United States Department of Agriculture (USDA) doesn't have rules regulating the labeling of organic foods for people or pets, although this will probably change in the future. Just because a dog food is labeled premium, superpremium, natural, organic, or gourmet, that doesn't mean it actually has to meet higher or different standards than other foods. If you're wondering, call the manufacturer—companies are required to provide contact information on their labels—and ask for specifics on what their claim actually means.

FIDO The Doggone Truth: All the Facts

All dog food labels must contain five pieces of information: the guaranteed analysis, which tells you the minimum and maximum levels of protein and fat the food contains; the nutritional adequacy statement; the ingredients; the feeding guidelines; and the manufacturer's name and address.

When it comes to generic foods, you get what you pay for, just like with everything else in life. Generic foods are priced low because they use poor-quality ingredients to keep costs down. Their nutritional quality is rarely confirmed through AAFCO feeding tests, and some may not even carry a nutritional adequacy statement. And because of the low level of digestibility, you have to feed a lot more of a generic food than a popular or premium food to ensure that a dog receives adequate nutrition, so you're not really saving at all.

Health Food for Dogs?

Nutrition plays an important role in overall health, and diet can be effective in managing certain conditions, such as cancer, diabetes, food allergies, or kidney or liver disease. Certain diets, known as veterinary medical foods, are formulated to meet these needs and are available only from your veterinarian. Because they have specialized nutrient content, they're not meant to be used as regular diets. Veterinarians supervise their use, so these diets are exempt from the AAFCO requirement that food labels include feeding directions. If this type of diet is prescribed for your dog, he might need to eat it temporarily or, in some instances, for the rest of his life.

FIDO The Doggone Truth: Don't Believe Everything You Read

You'll often see foods that claim to promote "healthy skin" or a "shiny coat." Know that this type of claim doesn't have any real meaning, however. Any good-quality food will give your dog healthy skin and a shiny coat.

Home Cooking for Your Pooch

Over the past decade, many people have begun to prepare their dogs' food themselves. Maybe their dog has a health problem that requires a special diet, or maybe they believe that they are using higher-quality ingredients in their home-prepared meals. Homemade food can be raw or cooked. Raw diets are popular because they're thought to be more natural and better at meeting a dog's nutritional needs.

> ### Doggie Dilemmas: Too Many Scraps Are Not a Good Thing
>
> Table scraps do not a complete doggie diet make. Sure, it's okay to break down and give him a bite of your food now and then, but stick to proper dog food for his regular meals. Remember, your meals are not formulated to meet a dog's nutritional needs.

Now, you probably don't need this book to tell you that the down side to preparing a dog's food at home is that it's difficult to produce a meal that's nutritionally complete, and it's time-intensive, too. Many people struggle to find time to prepare healthy meals for themselves, let alone their dogs!

If you're really into the idea of making your own dog food, choose a recipe from an expert source, such as a veterinary nutritionist. You can also find commercially available raw foods (usually frozen) at pet-supply stores, including "base" mixes to which you can add your own meat and vegetables.

Weighty Issues

It's all too easy to overfeed your dog, especially when his big brown eyes are pleading for just a little more. But as in humans, canine obesity is linked to health problems such as diabetes, heart disease, and joint aches and pains. Keep your dog at a healthy weight—it will help him live a longer life.

Canine Quick Fix: Simple Ways to Spot Obesity

When you look down at your dog, you should see a defined waistline behind his ribs. If Fido's just one big solid chunk of flesh, then he's got to shed some pounds. Check breed weight standards at the American Kennel Club's Web site, *www.akc.org*, to see what's right for your dog. If your dog is over the suggested weight range, doesn't have a waist, and huffs and puffs at the slightest exertion, it's time to start a diet and exercise plan!

Melt Away Those Pounds!

So you're ready to get your portly pooch into shape? Wait a minute—before you do anything, talk to your veterinarian. He can help you come up with the right plan for your dog. This involves considering his age, physical condition, and overall health. Regardless of these specifics, you can start by simply feeding your dog less. If you've been leaving out a bowl of food all day or giving heaping cupfuls of food, begin measuring portions and feeding meals at set times. Sometimes that's all you need to do. In other cases, you might need to switch to a lower-calorie food.

Also introduce more exercise into your dog's life. Start with short walks of five or ten minutes, depending on how out of shape he is. As his stamina improves, gradually increase the time and distance.

Time for Treats

It's pretty safe to say that dogs love treats. And what a dog considers a treat can range from pieces of his regular kibble to commercial treats to bits of hot dog, cheese, fruits, or vegetables. Dogs are pretty much happy with anything you give them to eat, but not all treats are created equal. Here are smart tips on treating:

- 🐾 **Keep treats special.** Offer them only as a reward; don't just hand them out indiscriminately.
- 🐾 **Limit treats.** They should make up no more than 10 percent of your dog's daily food intake.
- 🐾 **Read treat labels.** Avoid those that are high in sugar and fat, or give them only in small amounts.
- 🐾 **Vary treats.** Dogs like crunchy things, sweet things, and savory things. Offer bits of chopped apple, banana, or carrots, fresh or frozen berries, cubes of cheese or hot dogs, baked liver bits, and biscuits.
- 🐾 **Tailor the treat to the occasion.** Use tiny bite-size treats for training, larger biscuits or long-lasting chews for going into the crate or doing something else that doesn't require instant follow-up.

- **Know what's not a treat.** Certain foods, such as chocolate, grapes, alcohol, and onions, are all toxic to dogs.

The Well-Fed Dog

Not sure your dog's diet is the best it could be? Examining your dog's overall condition is an easy way to make sure of this. If you see the following things, your dog is eating well:

- Shiny coat with no hair loss or sores
- Healthy skin that's not itchy or inflamed
- Fresh breath, clean teeth, and pink gums
- Bright eyes with no discharge
- Clean ears with no redness or bad smell
- Small, firm stools
- Firm muscles and a visible waist behind the ribs

Don't be afraid to switch foods if your dog doesn't seem to be doing well on a particular diet. Remember, dogs are individuals, so a particular food, even if it has great ingredients, might not be the right choice for your pooch. Try a different brand or protein source (chicken instead of lamb, for instance) to see if you get better results. Just make the change gradually to give your dog's system time to adapt to the change.

Chapter 5

Basic Wellness

KEEPING YOUR DOG healthy is one of your most important tasks as a dog parent. With the help of your veterinarian, you can take steps to prevent health problems or to recognize them before they become serious. The key is watching for signs of good health or illness, knowing your dog's normal appetite and habits, and scheduling regular veterinary exams. And don't forget vaccinations and spay/neuter surgery!

An Ounce of Prevention

Okay, it might be a cliché, but that old saying about an ounce of prevention being worth a pound of cure couldn't be truer when it comes to caring for your dog. There are plenty of simple, common-sense things you can do for your dog throughout his life to make sure he stays healthy. Use a high-quality dog food with meat protein as the first ingredient, brush your dog's teeth frequently, make sure he gets plenty of exercise, dog-proof your home so he doesn't hurt himself, and protect him from disease with vaccinations. Pay attention to his eating habits; the condition of his coat, skin, eyes, and ears; how much he plays; and how much he sleeps. If you're familiar with all your dog's habits, you'll quickly notice when something's not right.

Watch That Appetite

Often, your dog's appetite is one of the most obvious signs of good health. The average dog is, well, a chowhound. Each dog is an individual, of course, and some dogs—and even some breeds—have a reputation for being picky. By and large, though, you can expect your dog to eat heartily twice a day (more often if he's a young puppy).

A Good—or Not So Good—Appetite

A dog with a good appetite reminds you when it's mealtime. She either dances around excitedly at your feet as you get her food or, if you've taught her good dinner manners, she sits impatiently, tail thumping, until you set her dish down and give the okay to dig in.

Now, on the other side of the spectrum, there's a difference between picky eaters and dogs who have lost their appetite. Picky eaters might "pick" at their food, only eating a little at a time, but they eventually finish it. Sometimes they eat well one day and refuse the same meal the next, having learned that they often get something different or special when they act this way. Other dogs are picky eaters until competition in the form of another dog is introduced; then they eat voraciously to protect their food from the newcomer.

Whether your dog is a chowhound or a picky eater, be concerned if you notice lack of appetite along with depressed or lethargic behavior, especially if it seems to come out of nowhere. It's not unheard of for dogs with healthy appetites to skip a meal occasionally—usually when the weather is hot—but if your dog turns up his nose at food more than once in twenty-four hours and just doesn't seem himself, it's time to take him to the veterinarian. Loss of appetite is often a sign of disease or dental problems.

An Eating Machine

Sometimes dogs eat more simply because they have increased nutritional requirements. Show dogs, pregnant dogs, dogs who participate regularly in canine sports, and dogs who hike, jog, or hunt frequently with their people need more food than the average canine couch-potato. They might also eat more in response to cold weather, especially if they spend a lot of time playing outdoors. These are all normal instances of increased appetite.

On the other hand, some diseases can cause a dog to eat more than usual. That's because the disease interferes with the way the body digests, absorbs, or converts food to usable energy. In other instances, it increases the rate at which the body uses energy. If your dog becomes ravenous, and the change can't be traced to a factor such as increased activity, see your veterinarian. This is especially important if your dog is eating a lot but still losing weight.

Doggie Dilemmas: Diseases Linked to Increased Appetite

Diabetes is among the diseases that can cause increased appetite. Others include diseases of the intestinal wall that interfere with food absorption and diseases that affect the hunger centers of the brain or that cause increases in hormones secreted by the adrenal glands.

How Well Do You Know Your Dog?

Pay attention to your dog's everyday actions. How she spends her days, her level of play and exercise, how she greets and interacts with family members, and even when and how often she potties will help you stay on top of her health. Consider keeping a diary of your dog's days. You'll find it's easier to spot changes in behavior or to see patterns if you can refer to a written record.

Play Time

Sporting dogs (retrievers, setters, spaniels, and pointers), terriers, most herding breeds, and some of the hound breeds enjoy high levels of exercise every day. Most other dogs, including some of the toy breeds, usually have a moderate energy level. They enjoy daily walks and playtime, but they aren't crazy bundles of energy.

If you have a high-energy dog, you'll know it if he's feeling lethargic. He won't want to play his favorite games or go for a walk or run, and his eyes might seem dull. Lethargy might be a little harder to spot

basic wellness

in a dog whose energy levels are moderate or low to begin with. But whatever your dog's energy level, don't ignore lethargic behavior for long. If he's uninterested in his favorite activities for more than a day, it's a good idea to take him to the vet for a check-up, because lethargy can be a sign of many different diseases.

Actions and Interactions

Changes in behavior and personality can also signal health problems. If your dog suddenly stops greeting you happily at the front door when you come home from work, take note. If your dog normally loves meeting people, be concerned if he suddenly shows no interest in them or even seems aggressive. Pay attention if your Labrador retriever turns away from tennis balls, your beagle stops sniffing anything and everything, your pug's tail loses its curl, or your Cavalier King Charles spaniel stops seeking out a lap.

Bathroom Breaks

It might not be what you thought you signed up for when you got a dog, but paying attention to a dog's elimination is a big part of keeping her healthy. Knowing your dog's normal patterns of urination and defecation allows you to notice quickly when they change. That's one of the many reasons it's a good idea to take your dog out to potty on leash instead of just sending her out into the backyard by herself to do her business.

The average dog will welcome the opportunity to urinate every four to six hours. If need be, however, most healthy adult dogs can go eight hours between potty trips. Male dogs tend to urinate small amounts in different areas, marking their territory. Females usually empty their bladders all in one go, although it's not unheard of for them to scent mark as well. Dogs normally defecate once or twice a day. Stools should be small and firm.

Signs of possible problems include changes in the frequency of urination, the amount urinated, whether the dog strains to urinate, and whether there appears to be blood in the urine. (Bloody urine is something you might miss unless your dog has an accident in the house and you see a pink tinge on the carpet.)

Doggie Dilemmas: Unexpected Accidents

If your perfectly house-trained dog suddenly starts having accidents in the house, don't scold him for breaking training. He might be trying to tell you he doesn't feel well. Take him to the veterinarian to check for any problems, such as a urinary tract infection.

If your dog needs to go out constantly and seems to be straining during urination, it could point to a bladder infection. Increase in the frequency and amount urinated, accompanied by an increase in water drinking, could indicate diabetes or kidney disease. Diarrhea can occur after a sudden change in diet or after eating garbage,

basic wellness

as a result of certain internal parasites, or as a symptom of a serious infection, such as parvovirus. If your dog is straining to defecate and is producing hard, dry stools, he might be constipated. All of these conditions require veterinary care.

The Value of Veterinary Checkups

Your veterinarian is your number-one partner in caring for your dog. If you're looking for one, get recommendations from shelter staff, breeders, and friends with dogs. If possible, check out the clinic and staff yourself. You want a clean facility that provides emergency coverage, with friendly staff who welcome your questions, and a reputation for good medical care.

An annual exam (plus visits as needed for illness or injury) will help to keep your dog healthy from nose to tail. During the annual exam, you and your veterinarian should talk about your dog's:

- Physical condition
- Vaccination status
- Parasite control
- Dental health
- Nutrition
- Behavior

If you've been keeping a diary of your dog's health and behavior, bring it with you. The dates and specifics in your journal can help your veterinarian figure out what's going on. Also be prepared to answer questions about your dog's habits. The better your veterinarian knows you and your dog, the better she can take care of him.

During the exam, the veterinarian will listen to your dog's heart and respiration rate; examine the eyes and ears; palpate (examine by touch) the body to check the condition of the internal organs and make sure there are no unusual lumps or bumps; and test your dog's joint and muscle condition by moving his legs to check his range of motion. You will also want to bring in a stool sample so the veterinarian can examine it for the presence of parasites. (See more about parasites in Chapter 12.)

Once the physical exam is complete, you and the veterinarian can discuss how your dog is doing and whether any changes should be made in his care. This is also a good time to mention any behavioral problems. If your veterinarian doesn't find an underlying medical cause for your dog's behavior, she should be able to refer you to a veterinary behaviorist or experienced trainer who can help.

Time for Shots

Nobody likes getting shots, but we all need them—dogs and humans alike. A vaccine is a substance that, when injected, provides immunity against infectious diseases caused by bacteria, viruses, and other organisms. It does this by challenging the body with modified disease organisms, provoking the immune system to form antibodies against those particular organisms. Vaccinations don't necessarily provide lifelong immunity and must be repeated at certain intervals.

 The Doggone Truth: Vaccine Effectiveness

Vaccines aren't always totally effective. They can fail if they are handled or stored improperly, if the dog's immune system isn't functioning well because of malnutrition or immunosuppressive drugs, or if maternal antibodies neutralize the effect of the vaccine. Nor will vaccines protect a dog that is already infected with a disease.

Are Vaccinations Always Necessary?

The decision to vaccinate a dog against a particular disease depends partly on the dog's age, breed, and potential exposure to the disease. It also has a lot to do with the distribution and virulence of the particular disease. Certain canine diseases are widely distributed, highly contagious among dogs, and serious or sometimes even fatal. Once a dog has acquired them, no treatment other than supportive therapy can help. These diseases are canine parvovirus, canine distemper virus, canine adenovirus, and rabies (which besides being fatal is also transmissible to humans). The vaccines against these diseases are referred to as core vaccines, meaning that they are recommended for all puppies and dogs.

Other vaccines are considered optional. In those cases, you and your veterinarian should discuss your dog's risk of exposure. The non-core vaccines are those against canine parainfluenza virus, Bordetella bronchiseptica (for canine cough, also known as kennel cough), leptospirosis, giardiasis, distemper-measles, and Lyme disease. Some of these diseases are not common in many areas of the country, so there's no reason to give them unless your dog is at risk. Your veterinarian can tell you which are necessary in your area.

When to Vaccinate

Puppies are vaccinated against parvovirus, distemper, and adenovirus-2 (canine hepatitis) at six to eight weeks of age, again at nine to eleven weeks, and at twelve to sixteen weeks, for the final series. A dog older than four months of age with an unknown vaccination history needs one dose of vaccine against these diseases. After a booster shot at one year, most authorities recommend revaccination every three years.

Doggie Dilemmas: Allergic Reactions

Reactions to vaccines are rare, but they can occur. Keep a close eye on your dog for the first few hours after she gets a shot to make sure she doesn't develop any serious allergic reactions. Keep Benadryl on hand, and ask your veterinarian how much to give in case your dog develops hives, swelling, redness, or itchiness. The vaccines that are most commonly linked to reactions are those for leptospirosis, rabies, and parvovirus.

basic wellness

The first rabies vaccination is generally given at four months. Boosters are usually given at three-year intervals, although a few states require annual rabies vaccination. Adult dogs with an unknown vaccination history need a rabies vaccination as well.

Recombinant Vaccines

A new type of immunization, called a recombinant vaccine, is created by splicing gene-size fragments of DNA from a virus or bacterium. The recombinant vaccines that have been developed so far—for distemper, rabies, and Lyme disease—are safe and effective. They work by delivering specific antigen material to the dog on a cellular level, reducing the risk of vaccine reactions, which sometimes occur with vaccines that contain the entire disease-causing organism. When recombinant vaccines become more widespread, it might be necessary to reconsider the age at which vaccines are first given, as well as the interval between vaccines.

Spaying and Neutering

If you don't plan to breed your dog—and you shouldn't, unless you have a superb example of the breed or you're a professional—have your dog spayed or neutered. Spay surgery, or ovariohysterectomy, is the removal of the female's uterus and ovaries. Neutering is the removal of the male's testicles, to prevent the production of sperm. Traditionally, spay/neuter surgery is performed just at or before the onset of puberty.

Many veterinarians like to schedule spay/neuter surgery at four or five months of age, when puppy vaccinations have been completed.

The Benefits

Besides its main purpose of birth control—sorely needed when there are already so many dogs out there in need of homes—spay/neuter surgery has health benefits. Females who are spayed before their first estrus cycle are much less likely to develop breast cancer later in life than females spayed after one or more cycles. They are also spared the risk of developing ovarian cysts or uterine infections. Neutered males have no risk of testicular cancer and are at reduced risk for prostate enlargement and perianal adenomas, tumors of glands around the anus. Dogs who are spayed or neutered are also more likely to get along better with other dogs and less likely to roam (unless they are scent hounds, in which case they are genetically programmed to follow tantalizing scents).

What You Need to Know

Before surgery, the veterinarian may recommend running a blood panel to make sure your dog is in good health. If your dog is young and has no known health problems, the only blood work will mostly likely be a simple test for blood urea nitrogen (BUN) levels, total blood protein, and a hematocrit, which is the ratio of packed red blood cells to whole blood. An aging dog or one who's not in tip-top health may need more extensive blood work.

basic wellness

75

The Doggone Truth: Surgical Woes
Scared about surgery? Don't be. Emergencies such as a reaction to anesthesia or a change in heart rate are rare. Thanks to improvements in anesthesia and monitoring equipment, veterinary surgery is very safe.

During surgery, the veterinarian or a staff member should monitor your dog's breathing and heart rate. Ask if they take the precaution of placing an IV catheter in a vein. This safety measure allows drugs to be injected quickly in the event of an emergency.

You'll also want to make sure the veterinarian provides your dog with pain-relief drugs before, during, and after surgery. Some veterinarians don't believe pain relief is necessary for routine surgeries such as a spay or neuter procedure, but more progressive veterinarians know that a dog who's given pain relief will rest better and be at less risk of tearing an incision.

What Happens After Surgery

During the first few days after surgery, your dog might be tired and a little sore, even with pain medication. Other dogs are as frisky as ever, running around and bouncing off the walls. Whether your dog feels well or not, keep him as still as possible. Rest will help the incision heal more quickly. You can limit activity by keeping your dog on leash or confining him to a crate.

Canine Quick Fix: Use the Cone

To keep your dog from licking or biting at her stitches, you might need to use what's known as an Elizabethan collar. This plastic, cone-shaped collar (which resembles a lampshade) fits around your dog's neck, preventing her from reaching the sutured area. Dogs hate wearing these collars and will often shake their heads in vain attempts to remove them. They sometimes run into furniture, too. But by and large, these collars do the trick.

Some swelling at the incision site is normal, especially if the veterinarian uses absorbable sutures. Depending on the type of suture, swelling may last for six to eight weeks. This swelling might be more noticeable on a dog with thin, delicate skin. Redness, obvious inflammation, or any discharge (other than a little pinkish stuff the first day or so) are signs of possible infection, and your veterinarian should take a look.

Medications

No matter how hard you work to keep your dog healthy, she's sure to need medication at some time in her life. Your dog's medication might come in the form of a pill, liquid, or drops for the eyes or ears. Before you leave the veterinarian's office, make sure you understand when to start giving the medication, whether it should be given with food or on an empty stomach, and how often you should give it each day. You should also inform the veterinarian of any herbal or holistic remedies or other medications your dog is taking. They might interfere with the effectiveness of the prescribed medication.

Whatever type of medication, it's important to give your dog the full course, even if she seems better after the first few days. Her body needs to build up a certain amount of the drug in the bloodstream for it to be fully effective. That's also why drugs need to be given at specific intervals.

Tricks for Giving Pills

The easiest way to give pills is to hide them inside a yummy snack. Peanut butter, cream cheese, and canned dog food are all excellent options for hiding pills. Before you do this, ask your veterinarian if it's okay. Some medications shouldn't be mixed with certain foods; for instance, tetracycline shouldn't be given with dairy products like cream cheese.

If you have a dog who eats the coating then spits out the pill, or if the pill should be given on an empty stomach, it's time for Plan B—giving the medication by hand. Hold the pill in your dominant hand, then use the other hand to hold the dog's mouth open. Place the pill toward the back of the tongue, close the mouth, and stroke the dog's throat to encourage swallowing. When you think she has swallowed, do a finger sweep inside her mouth to make sure she hasn't tucked the pill in her cheek to spit out later. Then give her a small treat or a few minutes of play with a favorite toy. The reward will encourage her to respond more positively to pill time.

FIDO **The Doggone Truth: Medicine Tactics to Avoid**

Don't crush pills and sprinkle them on your dog's food. Crushed pills can have a bitter flavor that might make her reluctant to eat, and you won't have any way of knowing if she gets all the medication.

Liquid Medicines

Most liquid medications come with a dropper for dispensing them. If they don't, you can use a plastic syringe (the kind without a needle), as long as it has the proper measurement markings. Fill the dropper or syringe with the appropriate amount of medication, and hold it in your dominant hand, using your other hand to open the dog's mouth. Place the dropper in the mouth, aiming it at the cheek pouch, and pinch the lips closed. Slowly release the plunger and continue holding the lips closed until the dog swallows. Follow with a reward.

Treatments for Eyes and Ears

Tilting the dog's head upward, hold the bottle in your dominant hand and squeeze the prescribed number of drops into the eye. Try not to touch the eye with the applicator tip. To apply an ointment to the eye, hold the head still with one hand, and pull the lower eyelid

basic wellness

79

downward. Using your dominant hand, squeeze a small amount of ointment onto the eyelid, then release the eyelid and gently rub the surface of the closed eye to distribute the ointment over the eyeball. Be careful not to poke the dog in the eye with the applicator. It might help to have someone else hold her head for you.

Ear medications often need to go deep into the ear, so they usually come in a tube or bottle with a long, narrow applicator. Place the applicator inside the ear and dispense the appropriate amount. Be sure you have a firm grasp on your dog's head while you do this. Before he can shake his head and send the medication flying, fold the ear over and gently massage it to make sure the medication is thoroughly distributed.

Part 2

Doggie Boot Camp

Chapter 6

Getting Your Dog to Go Outside

 IN PART 1, you learned some basics about your dog and caring for him. Now it's time to get to work—namely, training your pooch. The first order of business is house-training.

House-training is the most important lesson your dog needs to learn, second only, maybe, to the "Come!" command. If Fido never understands where it's okay—and not okay—to relieve himself, he can never be a full-fledged member of your household. If you want to be successful in your house-training mission, you'll have to be diligent about using a crate, establishing a routine, and keeping an eye on elimination behavior. Not to mention you'll need a decent understanding of dog physiology. You'll also need plenty of patience, and you'll want to use lots of positive reinforcement.

What's So Great About a Crate?

Crates are essential when it comes to house-training. Dogs are den animals, and their instinct is never to soil their den—in this case, the crate. Putting your dog in his crate when you aren't there to supervise keeps him from having an accident on your carpet.

"But putting my dog in a cage seems so cruel!" you might be thinking. No way—dogs appreciate having a place where they can relax and feel safe. What's really cruel is not protecting your dog from making mistakes and then punishing him when he does something wrong. Crate training is a positive way to show your dog what you want and prevent him from doing the wrong thing. This is much more effective than yelling at him after he makes a mistake.

You can encourage your dog to like her crate by making it a happy place. Besides sleeping in the crate at night, she can eat her meals in there, too. Every time you put your dog in her crate, give her a treat and say "Crate!" "Place!" or "Bed!" in a happy tone. Pretty soon, all you'll have to do is call "Crate!"—or the word of your choice—and your dog will scramble for her bed so she can get that yummy snack.

Too Much of a Good Thing

When it comes to the crate, don't overdo it. Except for nighttime, your dog should never spend more than four hours at a time in his crate. For one thing, he needs plenty of opportunities to exercise. Plus, if he's left in his crate too long, he'll have an accident inside it, which defeats the purpose of crate-training.

If you are gone for longer than the four hours, leave your dog in his safe room instead. Open his crate, put a couple of chew toys in it, as well as food and water dishes in one part of the room. Cover the floor with papers, so that any accidents will be easy to clean up. If you find that your dog consistently potties in a certain area, you can gradually take up the papers, leaving them only in the favored potty spot.

FIDO The Doggone Truth: Crate Doesn't Equal Punishment
The crate isn't a place for punishment. Never put your dog in the crate in an angry fashion. You want it to be a safe, secure place for him.

The Swing of Things

It's easy to predict when puppies will need to go to the bathroom. It's a safe bet that your pup will need a potty trip first thing in the morning, after eating and drinking, and after an energetic play session. Recognizing this routine will help you to set up a house-training schedule that will reduce or eliminate accidents in your home.

Set a Schedule

By taking your dog out at set times, he will learn when and where it's okay to go potty. A timer or alarm clock can help you remember to take the dog out at specific intervals. A good rule of thumb is to base the frequency of trips on the dog's age in months. A two-month-old puppy might need to go out every two hours, a three-month-old every three hours. Remember, though, that each dog is different and might need to go out more or less frequently.

Your dog will learn fastest if you stick to a given schedule instead of just taking him out whenever you think of it or whenever it's most convenient for you. If you're not home during the day, arrange for a neighbor or a pet sitter to come by and take him out at the appropriate time.

Tag Along

One good reason for having your dog sleep in a crate in your bedroom is so you can hear when he needs to go out in the morning. Take him out of the crate, escort him to the door, and put him on the leash. Walk him outside and let him sniff around. When he performs, give lots of praise in a happy tone of voice.

Why take him outside on leash? Because you need to make sure he really goes, and you need to be there to praise him when he does. Too often, people put their dogs out in the backyard and just assume they've eliminated. The dog comes in and immediately potties on the carpet, earning himself a scolding he doesn't understand. Your dog doesn't know why he's outside, so you need to be there to "explain" it to him by praising his actions.

Be Consistent

If your dog doesn't eliminate after ten or fifteen minutes, take him inside and put him in his crate. Try again in half an hour. Follow the same routine after every meal, after playtime, and before bedtime. Try to take the dog to the same spot every time. The lingering scent will prompt him to go there again. Spend some time playing with him before you go back inside.

Change the routine only if your pup needs to go out in the middle of the night. As soon as he potties, take him back inside and put him in his crate instead of giving him the usual playtime. You don't want him to start demanding playtime at 2:00 A.M.!

Canine Quick Fix: Stick to the Same Phrase

To help keep house-training consistent, make sure everyone in your family uses the same phrase when taking your dog outside. You don't want to confuse her!

As part of your dog's routine, he should be eating his meals at the same time every day. If you know when he has eaten, you'll probably have a better idea of when he'll have to go to the bathroom. On the other hand, if you leave food out all the time, you won't have any idea that he ate just before you got home from work and needs to go out now!

Feed breakfast after your dog eliminates in the morning. Space all meals about six hours apart. So if breakfast is at 6:00 A.M., lunch will be at noon, and dinner at 6:00 P.M. Most puppies will need to potty half an hour to an hour after eating. Start by taking your dog out ten minutes after he eats. If he doesn't do anything, continue taking him out at ten-minute intervals until he goes. This will help you figure out how soon after eating he needs to pee and poop.

On Cue

Pay attention to the way your dog behaves before he starts to eliminate. Some dogs circle, whine, or sniff first. Others assume a particular expression. Recognize these cues so you can hurry your dog outside when you see them. Get his attention and say, "Do you want to go out?" Don't wait "just until the next commercial." By then it will probably be too late.

Canine Quick Fix: Potty Preferences

Depending on what they're exposed to in puppyhood, dogs can develop potty preferences for certain surfaces, such as grass, gravel, or concrete. Try to expose your puppy to different surfaces, so he doesn't balk when faced with different options.

Accidents Will Happen

No matter how careful you are, accidents are bound to happen. That's just the way it is with puppies. If you catch your dog in the act, it's okay to say "Aaagh! Outside," but avoid using the N-word ("No") or saying "Bad dog!" It's the place he chose that's bad, not the act itself.

Anger and punishment only increase stress and fear, not to mention a greater likelihood of more accidents.

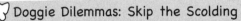
Doggie Dilemmas: Skip the Scolding

If you find a puddle or pile after the fact, simply clean it up. It's too late to scold. And never rub the dog's nose in the mess or swat him with newspaper. All that does is teach your dog that you're a big bully who attacks him for what is, after all, perfectly natural behavior.

Clean-Up Squad

Keep a good enzymatic cleanser on hand for puppy clean-up. These products contain enzymes that break down organic debris and waste. Products that do a good job include Resolve carpet cleaner, OdorMute, and Nature's Miracle. Look for them at your grocery store or pet supply store. Before using these products, test an inconspicuous area of the carpet (or other fabric surface) to make sure it's colorfast.

Avoid cleansers that contain ammonia. It's one of the components of urine, and the scent of it will draw your puppy back to the same spot. Stick to cleansers made specifically for cleaning up pet accidents.

When you find a puddle, use an old towel to soak up as much of the wetness as possible. Then saturate the area with the cleanser of your choice. Lay a clean towel on the spot and cover it with some heavy books or another heavy item. This helps wick the moisture out of the carpet.

For a pile of poop, use a plastic bag or a towel to pick up as much of the mess as possible. Spray the area with the cleanser and use a clean towel to blot up any remaining stool. Then follow the steps described above. When the area dries, it should be odor-free.

How Long Does Housetraining Take?

Remember that puppies are like human babies in many ways. Just as it takes months to toilet-train a toddler, it also takes months to house-train a dog reliably. Be patient during this process. Yelling at your dog when you find an accident only teaches him to sneak around and find secret places to potty. He might even avoid peeing or pooping in front of you at all, which really slows down the process.

Remember, too, that until he's at least six months old, your dog isn't physiologically capable of controlling his bladder or sphincter for long periods. The muscle control just isn't there yet, and it's not something that can be hurried along. That's why you need a crate and a schedule.

Never assume that your dog is fully housetrained until he's been reliable in the house for months without an accident. He might have occasional setbacks until he's a year old. If that occurs, make sure you still have him on a regular schedule. See if there are changes you can make to give him more opportunities to go outside when he needs to.

How to Housetrain an Adult Dog

The same techniques you'd use with a puppy are effective with adult dogs. The advantage is that an adult dog doesn't have to go out as often. The main thing he needs to learn is where you want him to go.

A schedule is still important, to give your new dog some structure in his new life. Dogs appreciate routine. Going out, eating, and playing at set times will help him adjust more quickly to living in your home. You can also crate-train an adult dog. Use the same techniques described for crate-training puppies. Again, a crate will keep your dog out of trouble and in your good graces.

Housetraining Problems

Puppies who came from an environment where they were accustomed to eliminating in a cage are often difficult to housetrain—so crate-training doesn't always work with them. Sometimes, they wait to eliminate until they're put in a crate, because that's all they've ever done. Working with this puppy calls for extra patience, as well as some creative thinking.

Canine Quick Fix: Housetraining Rewards

One way to teach a dog to potty outside is to reward the action in a way she'll remember. Take a clicker and some treats outside with you. As she pees or poops, click. When she's finished, give her a treat. Soon, she'll be anxious to potty for you when you go outside.

Supervision and Persistence Pay Off

If you've got a puppy who doesn't understand that he's not supposed to potty in his crate, try keeping him leashed by your side all the time. That way you'll be right there if he shows signs of needing to go out. Take him out as often as possible until he goes outside, and then heap praise on him.

If he messes in his crate at night, take him outside just before bedtime and try to get him to go. If he doesn't go the first time, take him out again in half an hour. Even if you have to go out several times, do your best to get him to go before you put him in his crate for the night.

Don't give up! It can take months before some pups catch on. By learning his schedule and understanding his body language, you can help teach him what you want.

When Rover Has a Relapse

If your dog suddenly starts having accidents in the house after months of being reliable, you should take him to the veterinarian. Many health problems, such as bladder infections, cause housetraining lapses. A physical exam and possibly a urinalysis or fecal exam can rule out any health problems.

If your dog gets a clean bill of health, study the circumstances surrounding the accidents. Has your routine changed? Is there a new pet or baby in the home? Insecurity can cause housetraining problems.

Make any reasonable changes you can to help your dog feel more comfortable, such as providing extra playtime or giving additional attention. You may need to go back to a strict routine of going out at specific times and confining him as needed until he's back on track.

Housetraining takes time. If your dog is having lots of accidents, review your schedule to see where you might be going wrong. Take him out more often, and don't forget to crate him or put him in his safe room when you can't watch him. Patience and a positive attitude will get you successfully over the housetraining hurdle.

Chapter 7

Basic Training

 MANNERS MAKE the dog, and teaching yours some essential behaviors is the key to rearing a well-behaved pooch. After all, you don't want Rover running your life! Basic training makes the difference between a canine holy terror who wreaks havoc and a cooperative canine who listens to you and is a pleasure to be around. Once your doggie dynamo settles down and learns "Sit," "Stay," "Come," and other commands, you'll be more confident in your relationship and able to take him anywhere.

It's All in the Click

A clicker is a small plastic box with a metal strip that makes a clicking sound when pushed and released. A clicker or other noisemaker (snapping your fingers or jingling a chain) serves as a bridge between the dog's action and a reward. Clicker training works on the principle of operant conditioning: the tendency to repeat an action that has a positive result.

Here's how it works: By using the clicker, you let your dog know what behaviors you like and signal that you will "pay" for those behaviors with treat or praise. For instance, you might click every time you see your dog chewing a toy that's hers—and not your favorite pair of shoes. Then give her a treat. After you've done this a few times, your dog will grab a chew toy every time she sees you coming. Once she catches on, you can add a word or a phrase that identifies the action you want, such as "good chew" or "good toy."

In training, timing is everything. The benefit of a clicker is that it instantly reinforces a behavior. A clicker also allows you to shape precise behaviors that might otherwise be difficult to teach—tilting the head, lifting a paw, or wagging the tail on command, for instance.

A Bit About Basic Commands

If you want to get going on the right training track, here are the five magic words your dog should know: sit, down, come, stay, and heel. You don't have to wait until puppy kindergarten to start teaching them, either. Your eight-week-old dog pup is ready, willing, and able to learn—so start practicing these commands.

Before you get started, pay attention to these simple rules:

- 🐾 Train when you're in a good mood.
- 🐾 Give commands in a firm tone of voice; praise in a happy tone of voice.

- ❧ Stop training if you get frustrated.
- ❧ Train in a quiet place with no distractions.
- ❧ Train before meals so your dog will be interested in the treats you're offering.
- ❧ Always end training sessions with something your dog has done successfully.

Be sure everyone practices these commands with the dog so he responds to all family members. This is also a good way to make sure he really understands a command.

"Sit"

"Sit" is a lifesaver. Use it to stop your dog from jumping up on people, to wait politely while you finish a conversation with someone, or to prevent your dog from tackling you before you have time to set down his dinner dish. "Sit" is also the easiest command to teach, so it's a good one to start with.

Get Started with "Sit"

To begin teaching "Sit," stash some training treats in your pockets or nearby where you have easy access to them. Take one treat in your hand and hold it just in front of your dog's nose. Slowly move your hand upward. As your dog's nose follows the trajectory of the treat, his rear should start to go down. As soon as he's in a sitting position, give him the treat and say, "Good sit!"

Run through this routine another three to five times. Any more than that and your dog might get bored. Wait an hour or so, and have another short training session. You can have lots of five-minute training sessions every day.

Canine Quick Fixes: Constructive Corrections

Ignoring your dog when he doesn't respond to a command is one way of giving a correction. Another way is to teach your dog a word or sound that means "Wrong, try again." Whatever word you choose, say it in a neutral tone. Avoid using the word "No," which has a negative tone and can discourage your dog from trying again.

As your dog catches on, start giving the verbal command without the hand signal. Give the command only once. If your dog doesn't respond, don't scold him; just walk away. Wait a few minutes, and repeat the command. Every time he responds on the first command, give the treat and lots of excited praise.

Teach "Sit" with a Clicker

Any time you see your dog sitting, click and treat. Wait to add a verbal command or hand signal (a raised hand) until your dog is sitting every time he realizes you have a treat in your hand. Just before he sits, give the command: "Sit!"

Once your dog understands that the word "Sit" and the action of sitting are linked, begin rewarding only the sits that you ask for. Again, if he doesn't perform on the first try, don't repeat the command. Walk away.

Practice "Sit"

Once your dog starts getting good at the "Sit" command, raise the stakes. Reward only the fastest or the straightest sits. Step away from him and expect him to remain in place. Gradually increase the distance you move from him until he remains sitting even if you leave the room. To increase the length of a sit, start to wait a beat before clicking. Also extend the amount of time between the sit and the click.

Practice sits in different parts of the house. You don't want your dog to associate the command with only one place. It's especially important to teach him to sit at the front door, in the kitchen before mealtime, and out in public (the checkout line at the pet supply store, for instance).

"Down"

This one can be a bit trickier to teach than "Sit" because it puts the dog in a submissive position, which many dogs prefer to avoid. Nonetheless, you do need to add this command to your bag of training tricks.

The classic way to teach "Down" is by placing a treat in front of the dog's nose and then moving it down between the legs and forward. (It can help to sit on the floor when you do this.) The idea is that the dog will automatically go into the down position in an attempt to follow the treat. If he does, say, "Good down!" and give the treat. Follow with the same techniques you used to teach the "Sit" command.

If this approach doesn't cut it, try the clicker. Click and treat every time you see your dog in a down position. Follow with the same techniques you used to teach the "Sit" command. Add a downward sweep of the hand at the same time you say "Down!" Soon you'll be able to give the command using only the hand signal.

Getting "Down" to Business

Once your dog knows this command, gradually increase the length of the down, just as you did for the sit. Any time he breaks the down and comes toward you, put him back in the same place and start over. Practice in different areas of the house, in public, and on different surfaces: the floor, grass, asphalt. Use "Down" when you're on the phone, working at the computer, or having dinner with the family.

"Stay"

Once your dog is a pro at "Sit" and "Down," you can start working on "Stay." Put your dog in a sit or down position. Standing next to or in front of him, place your hand in front of his face, palm up. Say, "Stay" (in a firm, less high-pitched tone of voice than the one you use for other commands) and back up just a few inches. Wait a couple of seconds and say, "Good stay!" and give him a treat. Then give a release word, such as "Okay," meaning that it's all right for him to move. If he moves before you release him, simply put him back in place and start over.

Practice Makes Perfect

Schedule a training session for the "Stay" command a few times each day. It's a good idea to practice this command when your puppy is already tired or calm. Try it after a meal, walk, or playtime.

Gradually increase the length of time you ask your dog to stay by just a few seconds—work up to ten seconds, fifteen seconds, thirty seconds, and so on. Start increasing the distance you move away from him as well. Remember, if he breaks the stay, put him back where he was and start over. You shouldn't scold him.

FIDO The Doggone Truth: When You Should Ignore Your Dog
Ignoring a dog's incorrect response is a form of negative reinforcement. Dogs like attention, so taking it away is a pain-free method of correction. It's much more effective than repeating a command five or six times in an increasingly louder tone of voice.

Time for a Distraction

When your dog has a good understanding of "Stay", start adding some distractions. Drop your keys, clap your hands, ask someone else to walk by him. Praise him ("Good stay!") and give a treat whenever he ignores the distractions and stays in position. If he breaks the stay, put him back in place and start over.

Gradually increase the level of distractions by dropping a treat or tennis ball near him, having someone ring the doorbell, or having someone walk another dog beside him. Practice indoors and outdoors so he'll encounter different types of random distractions (cars driving by, kids playing next door). Eventually your dog should remain in position until you release him—whether that's ten minutes or an hour later.

Canine Quick Fix: Backtrack When Necessary

Whatever command you're working on, pay attention to how your dog is progressing. If he doesn't respond or frequently breaks the command, don't hesitate to go back a few steps to the point in the training where he was getting it. Work from there to improve his mastery of the command.

He should also stay even if you're not in the room. When you're sure that his knowledge of "Stay" is solid, start leaving the room after giving the command. It's best if you have someone else in the room who can put the dog back in place if he breaks his stay to follow you. Wait thirty seconds, and then go back and praise him for staying. Gradually increase the length of time you're out of the room before returning, then have your assistant introduce distractions while you're out of the room.

"Come"

This one's important—in fact, it can save your dog's life if he's ever in danger. Use it to call him for dinner, to get him ready to go somewhere, or to get him out of the path of a speeding car. The "Come" command is easy to teach; the trick is making sure your dog responds to it instantly, every time. This takes time, consistency, and plenty of praise and other rewards.

Make This One Fun

Start teaching the "Come" command as soon as you bring your puppy or dog home. Puppies, especially, will follow you instinctively. Use this to your advantage by saying "Come!" every time your pup heads toward you. Use your most excited tone of voice, and reinforce the verbal command with body language by squatting down and holding your arms open. When the pup reaches you, give him lots of praise and petting. This is one command your dog just can't get wrong.

Gradually start calling your dog from a greater distance. Vary rewards so he'll always want to see what's going to happen when he gets to you. Besides praise and hugs, try an extra-special treat or a game of fetch. Practice this command several times a day, every day.

Put "Come" to the Test

When you're sure your dog understands "Come," start testing him in controlled situations. Practice in a confined area or make sure he's wearing a long line (such as fifteen- to thirty-foot clothesline) so you can enforce the command if he doesn't respond. Let him wander off. When he's no longer paying attention to you, give the "Come" command, using your happy voice. He should respond right away. If you call him and he doesn't come, wiggle the line to encourage him to come toward you (don't drag or jerk him), and give lots of praise when he comes.

 The Doggone Truth: Don't Scold!

Never call your dog to you and then scold him because he was doing something wrong (like chewing on your shoes). Praise your dog every time he comes when called.

If he's not wearing a leash, get him and walk him to the place where you gave the command, saying, "Come" as you go. When you reach the spot, say, "Good come!" Practice until he comes reliably no matter how far away he is from you or how interesting his other activity is. As his recalls improve, have him sit in front of you or at your side when he reaches you. When he's mastered that, reward him only for straight sits or only for very fast responses to the "Come" command.

To teach the "Come" command using a clicker, click every time your dog walks toward you, saying "Come!" as he heads in your direction. Click the instant your dog moves toward you and reward him when he gets to you. Start with very short distances of 2 or 3 feet, and gradually increase the distance from which you call him.

"Walk Nicely on a Leash"

Dogs love to explore on walks. Their noses are always sniffing out something. And, of course, there are other dogs to meet and interesting things to chase. That means going for a walk can be tough, especially if your dog is constantly pulling on his leash in search of the next best thing.

Believe it or not, your dog doesn't have to pull your arm right out of the socket—you can teach her to walk nicely on leash. She doesn't have to walk sedately at your side in a formal heel position, but not pulling is a must. There should always be some slack in the leash.

Hit the Road

To begin, attach the leash to your dog's collar. Hold it in your left hand with your dog standing by your left side. Encourage him to walk forward by saying, "Let's go!" (or whatever phrase you choose). Praise him or click and treat (or praise, then click and treat) when he starts to walk with you. He'll probably stop to eat the treat. When he's finished, begin again, this time clicking for more steps forward. Click only when the dog is moving.

Doggie Dilemmas: Pulling Predicaments

Sometimes, it's possible to inadvertently reward your dog for pulling—like when she pulls you toward people and then you allow her to greet them, or she pulls you into the park and then you let her loose off her leash to play. Before you allow her to do these sorts of things, make sure she's walking nicely!

As you walk, reward (praise or click and treat) your dog any time he is paying attention to you and not pulling. Gradually increase the length of time he walks before you give a reward. Vary the rate at which you give rewards so that your dog is motivated to walk nicely all the time.

One way to keep your dog's attention on you is to hold a lure, such as a favorite (small) stuffed animal or toy. Some dogs are crazy about feathers and will focus on those. Your dog will learn quickly that watching you is a good thing.

Any time your dog starts pulling, stop walking. When he looks at you and there's slack in the leash, you can start up again, reminding your dog to focus on you ("Watch me!") and rewarding him periodically as long as he's walking nicely without pulling. Stop and start again as necessary. If your dog is very strong and these techniques aren't working, you might have to try a head halter.

Practice walking nicely inside your home, in the yard, and around your neighborhood. Introduce distractions so your dog learns to stay focused on you. Schedule walks after a play session so that your dog has already worked off some of his energy.

Choosing a Trainer

Now, if you've diligently practiced all of the commands covered in this chapter, you're probably on your way to raising a reasonably well-trained dog. But let's be realistic here—everyone needs a little help sometimes. Sure, you could just head out to the bookstore or library and find the information you need to train your dog totally on your own. But isn't it nice to know that with some proper guidance, you can help your dog to learn things more quickly, so neither of you end up frustrated and you don't waste tons of time?

Especially if you're a first-time puppy parent, a trainer can help you understand what's normal and what's not, what behavior to expect at different stages of your dog's life, and how to teach your dog manners, tricks, and various dog sports. There are lots of reasons why working with a trainer is a good idea. Here are just a few:

- 🐾 **Experience:** Every dog has a unique personality and learns differently. A trainer who's worked with many dogs can try several different approaches to find out what works best with your dog.
- 🐾 **Socialization:** Training classes are great places for your dog to meet and learn to get along with other dogs and people.
- 🐾 **Attention:** In class, there's sure to be lots of stuff going on, so your dog will learn to pay attention to you amid distractions.

FIDO The Doggone Truth: Positive Training Only

Find a trainer who can help you bring out the best in your dog, using positive training techniques that make learning fun. Effective dog trainers use humane training techniques, such as clickers, praise, treats, and head halters.

Which Trainer Is Right for You?

Believe it or not, anyone can claim to be a dog trainer since no special instruction or certification is required. Check out credentials as you're looking for a trainer. Some have a diploma from a dog-training school or a degree from a university—in behavioral psychology or ethology (animal behavior). Whatever the educational background, a good dog trainer must have excellent communication skills and a thorough understanding of learning theory, training techniques, breed characteristics, general dog behavior and physiology, and human nature. After all, the trainer isn't the one actually teaching your dog: Her job is teaching *you* how to teach your dog. Here are some important things to do when looking for good trainer:

- 🐾 Contact professional dog-training organizations for member referrals.
- 🐾 Ask if your local club offers training classes if you have a particular breed.
- 🐾 Attend a class before signing up, so you can get a feel for the training style.
- 🐾 Interview the trainer about his or her experience and education.
- 🐾 Protect your dog from harsh training methods.

Canine Quick Fixes: Where to Start Your Search

Stumped about how to find a good trainer? Start by looking for one who belongs to a professional dog-training organization, such as the American Pet Dog Trainers, International Association of Canine Professionals, and National Association of Dog Obedience Instructors. Membership in such organizations indicates that a trainer's interested in continuing education, staying informed about advances in behavioral knowledge, and learning from others in the field.

How Does a Trainer Stack Up?

When visiting trainers' classes as an observer, make sure you're comfortable with their teaching style. An experienced trainer:

- Explains and demonstrates each behavior clearly before teaching it
- Explains and demonstrates how to teach the behavior, providing written instruction if pertinent
- Allows time during class to practice the behavior
- Spends time individually with students to work on problems
- Treats people and dogs courteously

Remember, dogs and people should have fun in training class. Steer clear of trainers with a drill sergeant mentality—unless you're looking to get yelled at. Training techniques have evolved over the years, and there's no need to jerk dogs with choke chains, or yell at them when they don't perform correctly.

Don't be shy about asking people taking the class about how they like it and whether they're happy with the progress they've made with their dogs. A six-week class should give you basic skills to work competently with your dog at home. Interview the trainer about his or her experience. Here are some questions to ask:

- How long have you been training dogs?
- How did you acquire your knowledge of dog training?

- How much experience do you have with my dog's breed?
- What training techniques do you find work best with dogs?
- Do you belong to any professional organizations?
- What will my dog and I learn in this class?

Don't forget—even if you find the best trainer in the world, you'll only get out of training as much time and effort as you put into it. So be prepared to work at it.

Doggie Dilemmas: Check for Vaccinations

Be sure the puppy kindergarten you choose requires dogs to be vaccinated and flea-free before attending class. Run the vaccination requirements by your veterinarian—some vets prefer not to expose puppies to strange dogs until the vaccination series is complete at four months of age.

Start Your Dog Young

Dog training used to start at six months, but puppies are capable of learning good manners much earlier than that. These days, puppy kindergarten is aimed at puppies ten weeks and older. The earlier you begin to train your dog, the more quickly you will develop a deep, powerful, and lasting bond with him. Puppy kindergarten is the perfect place to learn how to be your dog's leader and friend.

Look for a class with a manageable number of puppies, so the trainer is able to give individual attention to everyone. It's also a good sign if puppies are divided by size during playtime. Dogs play rough, and it's all too easy for a big dog to injure a small one accidentally.

What Happens in Puppy Kindergarten

A good puppy kindergarten class provides opportunities for puppies to develop social skills with dogs and people. You'll learn how to communicate effectively with your dog and cope with typical puppy behaviors, such as barking, play biting, chewing, digging, stealing food or trash, and jumping up on people. Pups learn basic commands ("Sit," "Stay," "Come," "Down," and "Off"), and how to walk nicely on a leash without pulling. Trainers might also cover such issues as spaying, neutering, grooming, health care, safety, and tattooing or microchipping for identification.

 FIDO **The Doggone Truth: Puppy Playgroups**

Some trainers offer regular "puppy parties" for socialization purposes. These informal get-togethers are a great opportunity for puppies to let off some steam, especially if they don't have another dog at home to play with or are alone during the day. Puppy parties have the same vaccination requirements as puppy kindergarten classes.

the "i have a life" dog owner's guide

The Next Step

In basic obedience classes, your dog will hone the skills learned in puppy kindergarten. The class might emphasize some especially important behaviors, such as stay, heel, and come. Again, the trainer will stress positive reinforcement, but you'll learn how to reduce or phase out the amount of treats you give. The goal is for your dog to learn to respond to your verbal commands and hand signals.

 The Doggone Truth: Continue Your Training

As your dog's skills improve, increase your standards: Require a straighter sit, a longer down, a come from farther away before you click. In this way, you shape the behavior to what you ultimately want the dog to do. With a clicker and the help of a trainer or a good book on clicker training, you can teach your dog all kinds of things.

Once your dog has the basics down, he can advance to more difficult lessons. These can include walking off leash, retrieving on command, jumping, scent discrimination games, and staying in position even though you've moved out of sight. Some trainers also offer classes designed for people who plan to compete in obedience with their dogs. In these classes, you'll be able to practice your skills in simulated conditions before facing a real judge in the ring.

basic training

If you and your dog enjoy basic obedience classes, there are other activities you can train for, including agility, flyball, and freestyle. Before you sign up for a sport class, be sure your dog is ready for competition—he should know and respond to basic obedience commands. Visiting people in hospitals and nursing homes is another option. To do this, you'll need to become certified as a therapy team. Organizations such as the Delta Society, Therapy Dogs International, and Love on a Leash offer certification programs.

Training Techniques to Remember

Remember, training techniques should always be positive, and the focus should be on communicating with your dog rather than forcing him to obey. Here's a quick round-up of key techniques to use:

- 🐾 **Praise**, to reinforce good behavior and let your dog know she's pleased you
- 🐾 **Rewards**, including a great treat your dog doesn't get every day, a special toy, or a favorite game
- 🐾 **Clicker training**, to help your dog make proper training associations and understand desired behaviors
- 🐾 **Head halters,** to allow you to control your dog's head, without causing pain, when he pulls

Canine Quick Fix: The Benefits of Head Halters

A head halter that fits well is a great way to teach a rambunctious pooch how to walk nicely on leash. The pressure a head halter puts on a dog's nose and neck evokes the same kind of neurochemical response that makes a puppy relax when her mother picks her up by the scruff of the neck or takes its muzzle into her mouth as a disciplinary measure. With the head halter, the dog relaxes and stops pulling, essentially correcting his own behavior. Then you can click and treat him for walking nicely.

Never forget that your dog needs positive motivational training if you want him to learn well. A dog who's forced or bullied into something will quickly become stubborn. Show your dog what you want and give him the opportunity to learn, and he will bend over backward to please you.

Chapter 8

Where Are Your Manners?

 BASIC TRAINING ISN'T all you need to instill a sense of canine civility. Your dog needs boundaries she can recognize. You don't want a dog who won't get off the furniture, drop things when told, or refrain from chewing objects that are off-limits. Show your dog that you're her leader, so you can teach her the household rules she needs to know.

House Rules

Wild and domestic dogs are pack animals who are guided by a leader and live by the rules the leader sets. Because your dog is living in a human household, you need to be his leader and lay down the rules. Dogs like knowing who's in charge and what the rules are, so don't let your dog down. Unless you set boundaries for him, he's sure to get into mischief.

Follow the Leader

Set rules by showing your dog what he can and can't do. Good leaders expect their dogs to behave in certain ways. Leaders don't get jumped on or knocked out of the way, and their dogs obey commands as soon as they're given. Leaders are in charge of food, playtime, and everything else in the dog's life. Here are some kind, effective ways to show your pooch you're top dog.

No Free Rides

Children learn to say the magic words "Please" and "Thank you" when they ask for and receive something. Your dog can learn to do the same thing by performing a command. When he wants to play fetch or tug, ask him to sit first. Then release him ("Okay!") for the game. When you feed him a meal, require him to sit or lay down before you give him the food. Again, he's not allowed to eat until you give the okay.

Have Some Respect

Your dog can show you respect by moving out of your way or waiting for you to go out the door first. If he's standing where you want to walk, ask him to move. If he doesn't obey, put a leash on him and move him where you want him to be. Then require him to sit or lay down until you release him.

Canine Quick Fix: Use "Down" to Teach Manners

As you're teaching your dog manners, "Down" is an especially good command to work on. This naturally submissive position can help your dog learn to accept your leadership and respond better to all your commands. Use it as often as you can during the day.

Teach your dog to wait before you go out the door, until you start walking, or until you tell him it's okay to jump in the car. Practice waiting at curbs before you cross the street. "Wait" is a variation on the "Stay" command and is taught in much the same way. You're simply using it in specific circumstances and giving it a different name.

Regular training sessions also help your dog understand his place in the family pack. They don't have to take long. Spending five minutes in the morning and five minutes in the evening working on obedience commands will do wonders for your dog's attitude. Don't forget to praise him for a good performance. Being a leader means letting your dog know when he's done a good job, as well as when he's made a mistake.

Give your dog attention on your schedule, not his. If he's constantly demanding attention, petting, or playtime from you by jumping up, nudging you with his nose, or pawing at you, teach him that you are the one who initiates these things. Either ignore his requests or—if you're inclined to grant them—require him to perform a command first. Crate him for an hour or two if you need to get things done around the

the "i have a life" dog owner's guide

house. Being in the crate gives him a chance to relax in his own space and keeps him out of trouble.

"Off"

It's cute when a puppy jumps up for attention, but a few months later when he's a bigger dog, it's not so cool. Here's where the "Off" command comes in—you can use it when your dog jumps up on people or you need to get him off the furniture.

FIDO The Doggone Truth: "Down" and "Off" Are Not Synonymous

Don't use the "Off" command interchangeably with the "Down" command. The words mean different things, and you want to avoid confusing your dog.

To teach "Off," you've got to move fast. When you see your dog is about to jump on you, say "Off," turn aside, and walk away so he misses his target. Then tell him to sit, and praise or pet him for doing so. Show your dog that he gets attention when he sits, not when he jumps up.

Another way to respond to jumping up is to ignore the dog (fold your arms, turn your head away from him, and stand like a tree) until he sits down on his own. The second he does, click and treat the desired behavior, saying "Good off!" This method works better with a puppy than a full-grown dog. Whichever method you use, your dog needs to learn that "Off" means four feet on the floor.

Keep Your Dog Off of Others

Lots of dogs like to jump on guests as they come through the front door. To put a stop to this, practice sits and downs with your dog at the door. Then ask family members or neighbors to get in on the act. Have them come to the door and knock or ring the doorbell. Put the dog in a sit/stay or down/stay and open the door. Praise or click and treat if your dog remains in place. If he jumps up, use your "try again" word and start over. Don't let visitors pet or talk to him until he performs correctly.

Be sure that everyone in the family knows how to respond to jumping up. Training must be consistent, or your dog won't understand what you're trying to teach. Avoid using unnecessary and painful physical corrections, such as kneeing the dog in the chest.

Doggie Dilemmas: No Exceptions with "Off"

What if other people say, "Oh, it's okay," when your dog jumps on them? Make sure that you explain to them you're training your dog not to do this. It's important not to make exceptions to your "no jumping" rule.

Some people enjoy having their dogs jump on them. They just want to be able to control when the dog jumps. When your dog fully understands the "Off" command, you can teach him to jump up on invitation. Pat your chest and say "Up!" When he responds, say "Good up!" Then give the "Off" command. Practice until your dog understands that it's okay to jump up only when you say so.

"Off the Furniture"

Once your dog understands that "Off" means all four paws on the floor, you can also use the command to keep her off the furniture. Firmly say "Off" and point to the floor. If she listens, praise her ("Good off!") or click and treat. Also say "Off" any time you see her getting off anything so that she learns to make the connection between her action and the command.

If your dog doesn't make the connection, help him off the furniture by luring him with a treat or toy, or gently guiding him with your hands or the leash, saying "Off." Then praise him or click and treat once he's on the floor. Use the treat lure only two or three times in the beginning, or your dog will start to demand a treat in exchange for getting off the sofa or bed. In this case, the treat's only purpose is as a lure to get the training process started.

To practice some more, encourage your dog back on the forbidden furniture by patting it and saying "Up!" This serves two purposes: It allows you to repeat the "Off" command sequence, and it starts the process of teaching your dog that it's only okay to get on the furniture when you invite him. As he improves, you can pair the verbal command with a hand signal, such as a sweeping motion of your forearm.

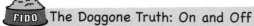

The Doggone Truth: On and Off

You can teach your dog that she's allowed on the furniture only when you say so. Before you invite her up, make her sit or lay down on command. Any other time you spot her on the couch or bed, use the "Off" command. You can also designate certain pieces of furniture as hers.

"Go to Bed"

This command comes in handy when you need to put your dog in his safe place before you go out somewhere or at bedtime. Use it any time you want your dog in his crate, on his bed, or in his safe room.

Every time you put your dog in his crate, say "Crate" or "Bed" in a happy tone of voice and give him a small treat. You can also click and treat, and say "Crate" every time you see him go into his crate on his own. Your dog will quickly learn that the word "Crate" means good things. If he's very food-oriented, it won't take long before all you have to do is say the magic word.

Use the same technique to teach your dog where his bed or safe room is. Say "Bed!" or "Place!" every time you see him there, and praise him ("Good bed!") or click and treat him for being there. Then

the "i have a life" dog owner's guide

practice giving the command and rewarding him when he responds correctly, or taking him to the designated area and repeating the command if he doesn't.

"Leave It"

Lots of dogs love to pick things up in their mouths. While this can be a good thing when you're teaching your dog to fetch, it's not so good when he starts to pick up things that could be harmful or that you simply don't want him to destroy.

Practice the "Leave it" command on walks. Any time your dog shows interest in something you don't want him to have, say "Leave it" in a happy tone. If he turns to look at you, click and treat him for paying attention and walk away from the object. If necessary, you can strategically place items you want your dog to ignore, such as food, socks, or shoes, along the sidewalk.

You can also use some extra-special treats to teach "Leave It" as you walk. When your dog stops to investigate something, show him the treat and then move it in the direction you want to go. When he follows the treat, say "Leave it" as you walk away. Give the treat when you're several feet away from the interesting item. Your dog will learn that "Leave it" means to move away from something. When your dog starts making the connection between "Leave it" and moving on, practice without the treat.

More Ways to "Leave It"

Here's another way to tackle "Leave it": Hold a good-smelling treat in a closed hand. Hold the hand out so your dog knows you have a treat. If he starts to sniff, paw at your hand, or nudge you in an attempt to get the treat, say "Leave it." Don't repeat the command, and don't open your hand. As soon as he stops trying to get the treat, say "Good leave it!" and give him the treat. Practice until your dog ignores the hand with the treat as soon as you say "Leave it."

> **FIDO** **The Doggone Truth: Advanced "Leave It"**
>
> You can eventually ensure that your dog will leave anything you tell her to. To advance training with this command, walk your dog closer to an object, add really desirable objects, or have a helper offer your dog food. Eventually, you can reward her for paying attention to you in the midst of something really tempting.

"Drop It"

To teach "Drop it," give your dog something he likes—maybe a favorite toy. Avoid giving him anything he shouldn't be chewing on in the first place. When he has the item in his mouth, take it in your hand and say "Drop it." If he lets go, give him lots of praise, then return the item to him. Let him have it again for a minute, then repeat the command. Practice with different things so he learns to drop anything you tell him to.

If he doesn't drop the item, gently remove the item from his mouth, saying "Drop it" as you do so. When it's out of his mouth, say "Good drop it!" Then return it to him and start over again.

Sometimes, a trade is in order. If your dog doesn't want to release a treasured item from his mouth, show him a treat or toy that he especially likes. If he drops the item in his mouth to get the new object, say "Drop it" as he does so, praise him and give him the treat, then give back the original item. From this exchange, your dog learns that he gets rewarded for obeying "Drop it."

"Wait"

Start teaching this command at doorways, either in your home or outside at the car. Take your dog to the door, and tell him to sit. Palm up in front of his face, say "Wait." Then start to open the door. If he moves, close the door and start over. Repeat until he remains in the sit position as you open the door. Click and treat every time he waits without moving. When you're ready, say "Okay" and let him follow you out the door or get into the car. Practice this command every day until your dog stays steady as a rock, and until you give the okay to move out.

Chapter 9

Socialize That Pup!

THE KIND OF DOG yours grows up to be depends in large part on how well you socialize him. The experiences a puppy encounters in his new environment are key factors in shaping his personality and temperament as an adult. Dogs are social animals and are naturally friendly, but they still need to learn about the different types of people, sounds, situations, and activities that they are likely to encounter in daily life. There are many things you can do and places you can go with your dog to socialize him—many of which we'll cover in this chapter, so read on.

Learning Begins in the Home

Your dog begins learning about his environment the minute he walks into your house. He'll have vacuum cleaners, blenders, doorbells, fireworks, and thunderstorms, and a host of other things to contend with. Be careful how you react the first time your dog encounters these things. He'll take his cues from your response.

FIDO The Doggone Truth: Never Overreact

Although first instinct is always to comfort a pooch when she's startled or afraid, whether your pup reacts to different, startling noises with fear or curiosity, be matter of fact. Don't comfort her if she seems frightened by a noise. Reassurance will only create a dog who's afraid of loud noises.

You and everyone in the family can start socializing your dog by giving him plenty of attention and affection. Introduce him to the neighbors and to delivery people. Invite neighborhood kids to play with him, and show them how to hold and pet him. Also, let your dog meet other dogs, as long as you know they are vaccinated.

Out on the Town

Walking your dog is important for his physical health and provides emotional release, but it's also a great way to introduce him to the things he'll encounter in your neighborhood: other animals, birds, kids on bicycles or skateboards, and more. A walk is also a good time to practice all those obedience commands you learned back in Chapters 7 and 8.

Close Encounters

As you meet people along the way, encourage your dog to learn how to walk up to people appropriately and greet them politely by sitting instead of jumping. If the person you meet has a dog as well, even better. Keep leashes slack so the two dogs can sniff each other without feeling tension at the end of the lead. You want your dog to look forward to meeting other people and dogs. Be sure your dog meets all types of people doing different activities. Also take him to a variety of places—outdoor shopping centers, pet supply stores, parks, and beaches.

Bright Lights, Big City

Urban dogs can have plenty of overstimulation going on, what with all the traffic, noise, and crowds of people they encounter every day. If you're a city dweller, get your dog used to these things early on. A dog who's startled by sudden noises or the approach of a stranger can bolt or get hit by a car. As soon as your veterinarian says it's okay for your pup to go out in public, start taking him on walks to expose him to the sights and sounds of the city. You can do this as early as eight to ten weeks of age, as long as he doesn't come in contact with other dogs and his paws don't touch the ground—carry him or put him in a crate and pull him in a child's wagon.

Doggie Dilemmas: Antisocial Canines?

A dog who doesn't love people might sound weird, but it can happen on occasion—especially if a pup isn't well socialized by the breeder. If your dog is shy around other people or dogs, help him develop more confidence and trust. Gradually introduce him to strangers and other dogs in carefully controlled situations.

Shy Guys

If yours is a shy dog, before you introduce her to someone new, lay down some guidelines. Ask the person to be still and quiet, refraining from petting the dog or making eye contact. Let the pup approach on her own terms, even if it takes a few minutes. Give her plenty of time to sniff and circle the person. When the puppy seems comfortable, the new person can slowly crouch down, to be at dog level. Let him or her offer the puppy a treat.

If your dog seems more confident after this introductory period, the new person can slowly reach out to scratch the dog beneath the chin. Don't let him or her try to pat the dog on the head, as many dogs view this as an aggressive move. Have the person continue giving small treats, so your dog learns that meeting people is fun and rewarding. Do this every time your dog meets someone new.

 The Doggone Truth: Don't Force a Fearful Dog
Never force your dog to go up to someone he's afraid of. Fearful dogs who feel trapped might bite. Even if he doesn't bite, your dog will lose trust in you as the person who protects him from frightening things.

Accentuate the Positive

Praise your shy pup for any willingness to approach a person, be petted, or take the treat. Ignore any fearful behavior. Whatever you do, resist reassuring the puppy with soothing words when he shows fear. This only encourages him to believe there's something to be afraid of.

If your dog is anxious around other dogs, start by introducing him—one at a time—to dogs you know are friendly and easygoing. It's best if the other dog is smaller than your dog, so he'll feel less threatened. As his confidence grows, gradually introduce him to bigger, rowdier dogs, and dogs of different breeds. Puppy kindergarten and obedience class are great places for your dog to interact with other dogs, under the supervision of an experienced trainer.

Play Dates

Even if your dog is well socialized, regular play dates with other dogs are highly beneficial. This is especially true if your dog is an only dog. Playing with other dogs helps burn off all that dog energy, and it's a great way for your dog to learn proper dog etiquette from older, more experienced dogs. A playgroup is also a good place for you to meet and talk to other dog owners and share information about behavior, health, and nutrition. It's nice to have a support group you can count on when you have questions about or problems with your dog.

Dog Park Do's and Don'ts

Rules and manners make life better for everyone—dogs and humans. Here are some guidelines to keeping things civil and healthy on play dates or at dog parks:

- ✤ Dogs should be friendly and well trained.
- ✤ Keep your dog on leash until you're sure of his behavior.
- ✤ Pick up your dog's waste and dispose of it appropriately.
- ✤ Don't let rough play get out of hand.
- ✤ Make your apologies and take your dog home if he gets aggressive or starts a fight.
- ✤ If your female dog isn't spayed, leave her at home when she's in heat.
- ✤ Bring water for your dog.
- ✤ Be sure your dog is fully vaccinated before taking him to a dog park.

Visits to the Vet

A visit to the vet is a great way to socialize your dog. The vet's office is filled with new people, strange smells, yowling cats, and barking dogs. Your dog will also have to get comfortable with strangers handling him. These are things that will give your pup's social skills a workout. There are plenty of ways you can help prepare your dog for this new experience so that it's a happy and not stressful one.

First, stay cool when it's vet time. If your dog senses that you're nervous about the visit, he'll pick up on your anxiety. If you and other family members have already been examining your dog at home by looking in his ears, examining his teeth and eyes, playing with his paws, and touching his tail and other parts of his body, he'll be more prepared for a veterinary exam.

Make sure your dog learns to be comfortable visiting the vet by taking him there early and often. Schedule a first visit just on a "getting-to-know-you" basis. The vet can examine your dog, but schedule shots for another time, so there's no painful association with that first office visit. Let staff members give your dog a treat or two to seal the new friendship.

Oh Baby!

If you have a baby on the way, should you be concerned about how your pooch will respond to this little newcomer? Don't worry. Dogs in the wild live in packs like families, and every pack member helps to care for pups. Like their wild cousins, domestic dogs love the family "pups," and they can accept babies willingly, if they're prepared for the new arrival. Begin introducing your dog to the idea of a baby months before your baby arrives.

Most dogs are curious about babies, which sound, smell, and look different from older humans. If possible, arrange for your dog to meet other babies so he can become accustomed to their scent, sound, and appearance. (You should only try this if your dog is well behaved!) With the consent of the parent, let your dog sniff the baby, so he can add "infant smell" to all the other scents stored in his brain. Don't hold the baby out to the dog, or he might try to grab at the little one.

Instead, sit cuddling the baby in your arms, and have the dog sit in front of you as he sniffs.

The Doggone Truth: Help with Change

Dogs are pretty adaptable creatures—they've had to be, to live successfully with us for so many millennia. Nonetheless, change is always tough for humans and canines alike, and everyone needs a little guidance when it comes to dealing with new situations. Welcoming a new baby into the home and moving to a new house are just two examples of changing circumstances where your dog will need your help to adapt.

Training Required

If you haven't obedience-trained your dog, do it before the baby arrives. A dog can accidentally cause injuries by jumping up on or running into Mom while she's carrying the child. Teach your dog to respond faithfully to "Sit," "Down," "Off," "Stay," and "Come."

Practice these commands while holding a doll or walking back and forth with it. Wrap the doll in a baby blanket and let the dog sniff it. Praise or reward your dog with treats for behaving calmly toward the "baby." Record the sounds of a baby crying or making other noises and play them frequently so your dog learns to recognize and accept them.

socialize that pup!

Canine Quick Fix: Scent of a Baby

Here's a good trick to get your pooch used to baby quickly. Send a blanket that has the baby's scent on it home for your dog to sniff before the baby actually comes home, so he'll recognize the baby's scent. When mother and baby come home, let your dog greet Mom first, without the baby. Introduce the baby and dog later, after your dog has had some time to assimilate the presence of the new family member.

Meet and Greet

To make the dog-baby introductions, put your dog on the leash and tell him to sit or down and stay. Keep the introductions gradual and controlled. If you're concerned that the dog might try to lunge at the baby, put a halter or muzzle on him first.

From a distance of 10 or 15 feet, show your dog the baby. If he stays calm, the person handling him can gradually walk him closer to the baby to get within sniffing distance. Again, don't hold the baby out to the dog; cuddle her close.

Keep your dog on leash for his first few interactions with the baby. Reward him for behaving nicely and calmly around the baby. You want him to associate the baby with good things. Once you're satisfied with the way he acts around the baby, you can let him in the room off leash.

Doggie Dilemmas: No Attention-Starved Pooches

Don't neglect your pooch after the baby arrives. Your dog is used to being an important member of the family—you shouldn't ship him off to the garage or backyard because you don't have time for him. Involve him in the baby's daily routine by taking the two of them for walks or letting him stay in the room in a down/stay or sit/stay while you're taking care of baby chores. With your help, your dog should adjust to the baby just fine.

A New Home on the Horizon

Relocating to a different city or state? There are steps you can take to help your dog become comfortable in a new home. First of all, visit the veterinarian to make sure your dog is up to date on vaccinations and in good physical health. If he's prone to carsickness, stock up on his prescription medication so he'll have a comfortable car ride or flight to the new location. And ask your veterinarian if he or she can refer you to a vet in your new area.

So what about when you get into your new digs? If the previous homeowners had a dog, your dog might want to mark his new territory. Before you move in, have the carpets cleaned to eliminate or reduce the scent of the previous pooch. This can also make short work of any fleas that might be hanging around. If possible, move

socialize that pup!

133

your furniture in before you bring your dog to the new house. He'll recognize the smell of your furnishings, which will make him feel more comfortable in the new place. When you bring him into the new house, take him first to his food and water dishes, and show him his bed or doghouse. Then let him explore his new yard. Maintain his old routine as much as possible during the move and unpacking.

Chapter 10

Model Behavior

 ALL DOGS—EVEN those who are smart, good-natured, and responsive to training—can have behavior problems from time to time. Wouldn't you know it, pups can be a lot like teenagers—many canines start causing trouble during adolescence, at six months to eighteen months of age. But behavior issues can creep up at any age. Fortunately, humans' understanding of canine behavior has advanced plenty in the last ten years, and there are many positive, successful techniques you can use to solve your pooch's behavior problems.

The Usual Suspects

You know the deal—there are a number of common unwanted behaviors your dog might engage in, much to your chagrin. No matter how diligently you try to train your dog, there's a good chance that Rover might revert to excessive barking, begging, chewing, digging, nipping, scavenging, and whining. Then there are other potential problems that can arise when pups get afraid, such as noise shyness and separation anxiety. And although less common, aggression is a possibility with some dogs, so you should be able to recognize and know how to handle it if it occurs.

If your dog's behavior gets out of hand, the most important thing you can do is remain patient. Continue to show him what you want, and provide firm, fair discipline when he breaks the rules. Read on, and you'll learn ways to manage or retrain your dog if he falls off the behavior wagon.

Canine Quick Fix: The Sooner the Better

Many of the above behavior problems can be easily solved if you build a strong training bond with your dog early in life. Let her know that you are her leader and that following you and doing what you ask will always lead to good things, and you'll be able to avoid problems or at least get her back on track easily when you hit a snag.

Aggressive Measures

In dogs, biting, growling, curling the lip, and other threatening behaviors all qualify as aggression. Although many breeds don't typically have aggressive tendencies, any dog can become aggressive given the right circumstances or poor temperament inherited from parents.

Where Aggression Comes from—and Why

Dogs can show aggression toward their owners, strangers, or other animals. Although it might not seem that way, most aggression is motivated by fear. Think about things from a dog's perspective, and it's not hard to see how certain situations could evoke fear in dogs and lead them to lash out. Here are some common types of aggression:

- **Conflict (dominance) aggression** usually occurs when dogs don't understand their place in the family pack or fear their position is threatened. They guard food and toys, refuse to move off the furniture, or display aggressive body language.
- **Fear aggression** relates to a frightening experience—anything from recalling a bad visit to the vet to associating the owner with something the dog is afraid of, such as fireworks. These dogs bite when they feel trapped.
- **Territorial, protective, and possessive aggression** occur in defense of what the dog considers his property: home, yard, owner, toys, or food.
- **Maternal aggression** occurs when strangers—or even family—approach a mother dog's pups.

Dealing with Aggression

Exposing dogs to plenty of people, places, movement (a hand throwing a ball or a toddler's awkward petting), and activities in early puppyhood can often prevent fear and possessive aggression. Practice taking away your dog's food dish or toys and giving them back. One way you might do this is by adding a treat to your dog's bowl, removing the bowl, adding another treat, and returning the bowl. Smart dogs learn quickly that letting you take the food bowl away is a good thing.

FIDO **The Doggone Truth: Facial Expressions**

Not sure if your pooch is smiling or snarling? Study his body language. If his lip is curled upward and his body is stiff and quivering, that's a sign of aggression. But if his lips are pulled to the side and his tail is wagging, that means he's in a friendly mood.

Puppy kindergarten, obedience class, and play dates at parks with other dogs and people are good ways to deter territorial aggression. These situations teach your dog that he must share neutral territory with others. Training helps your dog learn to defer to you as the family leader and protector of territory. Neutering at adolescence can also help reduce territorial aggression.

If your dog is behaving aggressively for no apparent reason, take him to the veterinarian to rule out a physical problem that could be painful. If that's not it, you might need to enlist a qualified behaviorist. Serious forms of fear or conflict aggression often require behavior modification, sometimes in conjunction with drug therapy.

Barking up the Wrong Tree

Dogs don't speak words, but they do have their own way of communicating vocally. Dogs bark in greeting, to warn intruders off their territory, in excitement, or out of stress or boredom. They might whine for attention or because they're in pain.

It's okay for your dog to bark or whine, but only in appropriate circumstances, which might include welcoming you home from work, alerting you to the presence of someone approaching the house, or in warning because of a fire or other danger. With training, your dog can learn when it's okay to bark and when not to raise a ruckus.

Barking the Right Way

Start training the first day your dog comes home with you. If he barks when someone comes to the door (either before or after they knock or ring the doorbell), praise him for his alertness. If he doesn't bark, help him get into the spirit of things by saying, "Who's there? Who is it?" Do the same for any other situations when you do want your dog to bark.

When your dog has learned to alert you to people approaching the house, teach him how to be quiet. Let him bark once or twice, then say, "Enough" or "Quiet." Your voice should distract him enough so he stops barking. If he does, say "Good quiet," and give him a treat. Gradually extend the length of time between his silence and giving him the treat. Use the same technique to stop whining.

The Barking Fix

If your dog won't quit barking, try calling him or giving him a down command, to distract him. When he's quiet, praise him and give a treat. You might also try a squirt from a spray bottle to deter his boisterous behavior. Whatever you do, avoid loud verbal corrections. Your dog might just decide you're barking along with her and then bark even more loudly!

What if your dog barks too much for no reason? First, understand there's always a reason. Is he bored because he's alone all day? Are the squirrels in the yard taunting him? Is he mouthing off at all the delivery people who come down the street during the day? It's your job to figure it out.

FIDO **The Doggone Truth: Don't Inadvertently Reinforce Barking**
Never reward your dog for barking unless it's a situation where you actually do want him to bark. If you let him out of his crate and toss him his ball right after he barks at you, you're inadvertently reinforcing and rewarding his behavior. Wait until he's quiet for at least thirty seconds before you give him what he wants. The same goes for whining.

Never punish your dog for barking because she's bored. If she's barking because she's outside, it's because she wants company. You need to bring her in the house. (Wouldn't you get lonely too if you were left outside alone?) If your dog barks during the day because he's bored while you're gone, rotate his toys so he always has something new. You can also give him a goodie bag full of treats he has to work at to get into. Use a paper bag, fill it with toys and treats, and tape it closed. Give it to your dog before you leave for work. He'll be so busy getting into it that he won't have time to bark.

What to Do with a Whiny Pup?

Dogs whine when they want something, when they're frustrated or excited, or when they're in pain. Make sure to know what's causing your dog's whining. If he is whining out of frustration or for attention, don't offer a verbal correction. Instead, ignore the behavior and distract him with some other activity, such as practicing commands. If you know your dog is in pain, comfort him and give him affection and attention. Contact a veterinarian if you suspect there's something seriously wrong with him.

You Little Beggar

There's one really simple solution for begging: Don't let it start in the first place. Never feed your dog from the table or offer him scraps while you're cooking, or else she'll be constantly underfoot, hoping for a tidbit.

If your dog is a shameless beggar, give him his meal before the family eats. His hunger will be assuaged, and he'll be less likely to bother you at the dinner table. If you let him in the room while the family is eating, put him in a down/stay. Do the same thing if he likes to hang out in the kitchen while you're cooking. Choose a corner away from where you're working, and make sure he stays there.

Besides begging for food at the dinner table, all dogs love to raid the trash. The best way to deal with a scavenger is to run interference. Place contact paper (sticky side up) over the top of the trash, keep the trash behind closed doors (store it beneath the kitchen sink and put child locks on cabinets) or use a can with a tightly fitting lid that your dog can't remove. Problem solved.

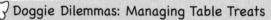

Doggie Dilemmas: Managing Table Treats

What if you're a sucker who just can't resist giving your dog a snack while you're making a meal? Do you have any hope of controlling begging? Yes, if you make her sit or lay down first before treating and then send her back to her place. And only give treats when you've told your dog to come.

If that doesn't cut it, make getting into the trash counterproductive. If your dog enjoys playing with empty paper towel rolls—which can make great dog toys—and pulls one out of the trash, take it away. Later, you can give him a different roll to play with. Eventually he'll learn that paper towel rolls that come from you are fair game; those raided from the trash get taken away.

Chew Fest

Young dogs have a physiological need to chew; it's simply part of their development. Older dogs might continue the chewing habit simply because it's enjoyable. Chewing is a way to pass the time when there's nothing else to do. Since you know your dog is likely to chew no matter what, it's your job to provide him with a variety of acceptable chew toys, as well as to teach him what not to chew.

Good Chewing Habits

You can teach your dog to chew the right things by praising him every time you see him gnawing on a toy. Help make toys even more appealing by handling them frequently so they hold your scent. Your dog wants to be close to you, even when you're not home, so chewing on something that smells like you is the next best thing. That's often why dogs chew up their owners' favorite shoes or clothes. No, it's not out of spite—it's out of love.

You can also up the appeal of certain toys, like a Kong or hollow rubber bone, by filling them with treats. Fill with peanut butter and stuff in small biscuits or baby carrots.

The Chewing Stops Here

The two best ways to prevent inappropriate chewing are to put your things out of reach and to leave your dog in his crate or safe room when you can't be there to supervise. That way, your possessions don't get destroyed, and your dog doesn't get scolded for misbehaving. Just make sure he has something nice to chew on when he's confined.

When you catch your dog chewing something he shouldn't, give an immediate verbal correction: "Aaaght" or "No!" If he's chewing on something life-threatening, such as an electrical cord, instantly follow the verbal correction with a squirt from a spray bottle. Your dog needs to learn that there are serious consequences to chewing on cords—before he gets electrocuted.

If he's chewing on something not so dangerous—but still forbidden—give the same verbal correction. That should be enough to distract him. When he stops chewing to look at you, give him a toy to chew on instead. Don't forget to praise him every time you see him chewing on something appropriate.

Ditch the Inappropriate Digging

Digging is a normal behavior for dogs. In the wild, dogs dig to make a bed, find prey, or hide a food stash. Domesticated dogs dig primarily for entertainment, although an ancestral impulse might be at work as well. The point is that your dog isn't digging to annoy you; he's just occupying himself while you're gone. Fortunately, there are ways to solve the digging dilemma.

Digging Deterrents

One way to prevent digging is to provide your dog with more exercise and playtime. Your goal is to get him too tired to dig. When that's not possible, make sure he has plenty of interesting toys that are more fun than digging. Look for a Giggle Ball or Buster Cube. Giggle Balls make—naturally—a giggling sound when they're pushed, and Buster Cubes can be filled with treats, which the dog can get at by manipulating the cube. Stuff a large Kong with treats, and leave out a soccer ball or a supply of tennis balls.

Redirecting digging is another option. Give your dog his own sandbox or dirt pile where he can dig to his heart's content. Define it with a border of railroad ties and stud it with toys or rawhides that he can dig up and enjoy. Whenever you see your dog digging in a forbidden area, distract him by saying "Aaaght" or "Leave it," and then show him his digging spot. When he digs there, give lots of praise: "Good dig!" Reward him every time you see him digging in the right spot.

Canine Quick Fix: Fill Those Holes

If your dog digs in inappropriate spots, try filling the holes with rocks, gravel, or pine cones, so it's no longer comfortable for her to dig there.

For a dog who likes to dig in your garden, put a picket fence or chicken wire around it to deny him access. You might also want to

model behavior

consider surrounding the garden (or other favored digging spot) with a new type of electronic fence. The dog must wear a special collar that activates whenever he crosses the boundary, giving off a burst of citronella spray. Dogs don't like the smell of citronella, so this type of fence offers a self-correcting method of preventing digging in specific areas.

A Change of Scenery

Is your dog digging to make a cool spot when it's hot outside? Consider moving his doghouse to a shadier area, and get him a plastic kiddie pool to splash in. If all else fails and your yard is starting to look like a minefield, keep your dog indoors when you can't be there to supervise. Another option is to build a dog run in the yard where he can be confined when you're not home. Give the run a concrete base to prevent him from digging beneath the fencing.

A Mouthy Dog

While dogs use their mouths for a bunch of important things—like picking up, carrying, and tasting things or defending themselves or objects they perceive as theirs—your dog must learn that he shouldn't use his teeth on people. In some places, a single dog bite is enough to require a dog to be euthanized, so teaching your dog not to mouth or bite people is a must.

A puppy's lessons in how to use his mouth and teeth begin with his littermates and mother. They yelp loudly or cuff him with their paws if he bites too hard. You can continue that lesson by screeching loudly and then walking away any time your pup bites down too hard on your hand. Remember, dogs hate being ignored.

Help your dog develop gentle habits by offering tiny treats held in your fingers. If he bites down too hard, yell "Ouch" and walk away with the treat. Try again in a couple of minutes and repeat until he learns how to take food gently. This technique also works during games of fetch or tug.

Noise Shyness

Loud noises startle most of us, but we usually jump a little and then go about our business. Some dogs, however, develop a debilitating fear of thunder, fireworks, gunshots, and other loud noises. Noise-shyness in dogs is distressing because it often leads to destructive behavior or a dog who runs away and gets lost or hurt. You can, however, help your dog overcome his fear of loud sounds.

How to Handle It

First and most important, don't cuddle or talk soothingly to your dog while he's displaying fearful behavior. By doing that, you'll reinforce the idea that there's something to be afraid of. Behave normally and ignore the dog's behavior. On the flip side, don't force your dog to be around the noise or punish him for behaving fearfully; both actions can make the problem worse.

Watch if your dog heads for a safe place whenever loud noises occur, then make sure he has easy access to it if a storm is brewing or dusk is falling on the Fourth of July. Don't lock him up in the safe place, whether it's a crate or a room. He should be free to leave it if he wants to.

Distraction can work well, too. Try using it when there are signs of a thunderstorm, but your dog hasn't yet tried to hide or started to whimper. Play a game of tug or fetch—inside—or practice some obedience commands, and give lots of praise and rewards. Just be sure to stop the game or training if your dog starts acting afraid, and let him go to his safe place if he chooses.

Behavior Modification

Counterconditioning and desensitization are behavior modification techniques that can help dogs overcome fears. They involve gradually getting the dog accustomed to sounds (or other stimuli) that cause fear and replacing the fearful response with one that's more acceptable. Like most behavior modification, these techniques require time and patience.

Get a recording of thunderstorm noises or make a recording of firecracker sounds or whatever noise frightens your dog. Play the recording at a very low volume, so that it's almost inaudible. While the recording is playing, do something your dog enjoys. Play fetch, give treats, or feed a meal.

Do the same thing each time you play the recording. Over a period of days, weeks, or months, gradually increase the volume. If you notice your dog starting to display fearful behavior, stop the recording. Try again later at a lower level. Eventually, your dog should start to associate the frightening sound with good times.

If your dog is extremely fearful of noises, talk to your veterinarian about getting a short-term prescription of an anti-anxiety drug for her. Medication alone won't solve the problem, but it can help the behavior modification process. Working with a behaviorist might be helpful, too.

Separation Anxiety

Separation anxiety is a panic response that occurs in a dog when his family members leave home. Dogs with separation anxiety become highly distressed, usually within an hour of the person's departure. They sometimes dig, chew, or scratch at doors or windows in an attempt to get out and find their caregivers. They might also howl, bark, whine, or lose control of their bowels or bladder.

The trick here is gradually getting your dog accustomed to being left alone. Start by teaching your dog there's no need to freak out during brief absences. Practice by doing all the things you would normally do before leaving: Get your purse or wallet, pick up your keys, and put on your coat. Don't leave. Repeat this several times over several days until your dog can handle this.

Gradually up the ante: Step outside, close the door, and come right back in; leave, close the door, wait a few seconds, and come back in; and so on. Eventually, practice leaving for short periods. Say "I'll be back" to let your dog know you're leaving. Step outside the door, close it, and wait one minute. Then re-enter in an unconcerned manner. You can greet your dog quietly or just ignore him.

Practice leaving and returning at different times of the day. Your dog needs to learn that it doesn't matter what time you leave; you'll always come back. Once he's comfortable with your absence for thirty to ninety minutes, you can jump up to longer intervals, such as half a day.

Part 3

Canine Health Concerns

Chapter 11

Is Your Dog Ill?

 BEING A MEMBER of the family, your dog counts on you to care for and help her when she's sick. At the same time, dogs retain enough of their "wild" side to often cover up signs of illness. In any case, it's your job to provide good preventive health care and also observe your dog closely so you can recognize what she's like in her normal, healthy state, and how she behaves when she's not feeling so hot. Following is a quick list of ailments to watch for, as well as a rundown on pain as it relates to your pooch.

Bleeding

The only time bloody discharge is normal is in unspayed female dogs at the proestrus stage of their heat cycle. A bloody drip from the vulva of a spayed female or from the penis of a male might indicate a bladder infection. Blood from the vulva of an unspayed female dog who is not in heat could indicate an overgrowth of uterine lining or a uterine infection—both potentially life-threatening.

Bloody discharge from the mouth could be as simple as a small cut on the gums or tongue or as silly as a lost baby tooth for a puppy. Coughing up blood is a bad sign and requires immediate veterinary attention.

Doggie Dilemmas: Head to the Vet!

Bloody discharge, including spurting blood from an artery, coughing up blood, or blood from the vulva of an unspayed dog not in heat can be an emergency. Apply pressure to any spurting areas, and head straight to your vet!

Blood in stool can be black with digested blood from a problem such as a stomach ulcer, or bright red from a bleeding problem in the intestines. Bloody discharges from any part of your dog's body might indicate cancer or a bleeding disorder such as autoimmune hemolytic anemia or von Willebrand's disease, a blood-clotting disorder caused by a genetic deficiency.

What to Do

A bloody nose might need pressure and/or a cold compress, either of which is applied to the top of the nose. Bleeding from the mouth is also easy to care for if it's from a lost baby tooth; put a cold compress on the spot or just wait it out. The bleeding should stop fairly quickly. Under most circumstances, however, blood is a good indicator that

is your dog ill?

you need to have your dog checked out. If you see blood in your dog's urine or stool, get her to a veterinarian. If possible, scoop up a sample. Any bleeding associated with a growth or tumor should get veterinary attention as well.

Breathing Trouble

Normally dogs take ten to thirty breaths per minute. This varies with temperature, activity, and size of the dog. In hot weather, a normal dog might pant up to 200 times per minute. A dog who is breathing faster than normal might be taking shallow breaths that aren't as efficient at moving oxygen into the lungs. If your dog seems to be working to breathe, not just breathing naturally, something is wrong.

Difficulty breathing can have a number of causes. A dog in pain often has quick, shallow breathing. Any abdominal problem that puts pressure on the diaphragm can cause respiratory difficulty as well. A dog who has been hit by a car or had other trauma might have broken ribs or what is called a pneumothorax (free air in the chest, putting pressure on the lungs). Pneumothorax is a serious, potentially life-threatening problem that requires immediate veterinary care.

Respiratory Problems

A dog with a respiratory infection might have purulent (pus-filled) discharge from the nose that blocks his airways. Any obstruction in the nose—blood clots from banging the nose on something hard, inhaled foreign objects, or tumors—can reduce the amount of air going into the lungs. The same holds true for all the airways down to the lungs.

Pneumonia and Other Lung Problems

Once air gets down to the lungs, other problems can arise. Pneumonia is an infection of the lungs by either viruses or bacteria. It can be quite serious, especially in puppies or dogs with poor immune systems. Dogs with pneumonia might cough, gag, retch, or just have painful breathing. These dogs usually show other signs of illness such as a fever or poor appetite, and they might cough up greenish mucus.

Pneumonia can also be caused by parasite migrations, such as with roundworms, or if the dog inhales bits of food into the lungs. If your dog has pneumonia, your veterinarian might perform a process known as a tracheal aspirate. This involves injecting sterile fluid into the trachea, then sucking it back out into a syringe so it can be cultured and examined. X-rays are also important in diagnosing pneumonia.

Excessive Drinking

Dogs sometimes drink more than usual for a number of reasons, such as being active or out in the hot sun. However, some health problems can cause an increase in drinking too.

Any situation that might dehydrate your dog will lead to increased drinking. Diarrhea and vomiting take a lot of fluid from your dog, and it must be replaced. Fever or mild heat stroke can stimulate dogs to drink more than usual, as can bladder infections and mild kidney problems. More serious problems like kidney failure can also lead to increased drinking and urinating, or sometimes to a drop in drinking and little urine production.

 The Doggone Truth: Water Requirements

Dogs need about 10 ml of water per pound of body weight daily. Activity, environment, or health problems can all increase the amount needed. Ideally this will come from fresh water, but if your dog is ill, she might need intravenous fluid replacement.

Certain hormonal diseases directly influence the amount your dog drinks. With diabetes mellitus, for instance, either the pancreas doesn't produce enough insulin or the insulin present isn't working properly to remove extra glucose from the blood. A diabetic dog therefore drinks more water to flush out extra glucose.

Dogs who suffer from Cushing's disease (excessive adrenal secretions) or from Addison's (not enough adrenal secretions) sometimes show increased thirst. Female dogs with pyometra (uterine infections) will often be very thirsty, and dogs with increased calcium in the blood are also very thirsty.

What to Do

First off, make sure water bowls are always available and refill them with fresh water at least twice daily. Just like humans, dogs prefer fresh, cool water. Pay attention to whether you need to fill the bowl up more often than usual. If you're concerned about changes in drinking habits, be sure to let your veterinarian know. He might need to do some blood work, including tests requiring a short hospital stay, to measure how much your dog is drinking and how much urine is being produced.

Unexplained Weight Loss

Weight loss occurs in one of two ways—either insufficient calories are being taken in, or extra calories are being burned. If your dog's appetite and eating habits are still normal, the extra energy is being used somehow, if not with exercise then possibly with a great metabolic use of calories.

Diabetes mellitus is one example of a disease with which a dog might have a good (if not voracious) appetite but still lose weight. This disease affects the production of insulin so the dog can't use all the calories consumed.

What to Do

Because the causes of weight loss can be so serious, be sure to get it checked out. Certainly, an unexplained weight loss of 10 percent of your dog's body weight is cause for a veterinary visit. Your veterinarian will want to check a fecal sample for parasites that can drain nutrition, then possibly do some blood work or check for abnormalities with X-rays or an ultrasound.

Coughing and Sneezing

An occasional cough or sneeze is not cause for alarm. Some of the worst-sounding coughs are actually caused by respiratory viruses known as canine cough or kennel cough. These are usually not serious and are easy to treat. Coughing might also be the result of something simple like inhaling water. But coughing could also be a sign of a serious problem, such as cancer or pneumonia. Heart problems that allow fluid to build up in the lungs might be accompanied by a cough as well. Dogs can snort up grass or bugs, or they might develop cancerous growths that block nasal passages and cause repeated sneezing.

What to Do

If your dog is sneezing repeatedly, possibly even to the point of sneezing a few blood droplets, investigate the cause. Also check into any sneezing with a thick or discolored discharge. Your dog might need to visit the veterinarian, who will carefully look into the dog's nose with a special scope.

Dogs with a chronic cough will need a full veterinary workup. This could include blood work, X-rays, and possibly an ultrasound or an examination of the airways with an endoscope. The veterinarian might decide to perform a needle biopsy, which involves removing a small sample of cells for examination, or a tracheal wash: The trachea is washed with sterile fluid, which is then checked for any unusual cells. Treatment for coughing problems might include oxygen therapy, cough suppressants, or antibiotics.

Eye, Ear, and Nose Problems

Your dog's eyes, ears, and nose are all sensitive areas with plenty of specialized nerve endings to help in seeing, hearing, and smelling. Any discharges from these areas might interfere with your dog's keen senses and could indicate a deeper problem.

 The Doggone Truth: What's Entropion?

Some breeds are prone to entropion, a condition that causes eyelids to turn in so that hairs rub on the cornea. This is most common in dogs with shortened faces and long facial hair such as Shih Tzus and breeds with wrinkled skin like bulldogs and Shar-Peis. These breeds might need special surgery to prevent eye problems.

Recognizing Eye Problems

Normally, your dog's eyes should be bright and clear with no discharge. A clear discharge might mean a mild irritant (dust or pollen in the eye) or a hair rubbing against the sensitive cornea. Any discolored or thick discharge such as pus or heavy mucus is abnormal and cause for alarm. Eye problems can go from minor to serious very quickly. If your dog has a discharge and is squinting, he needs to see a veterinarian!

Recognizing Ear Problems

Dogs with ears that hang down and prevent air circulation might have a slightly musty odor, but there should never be a foul odor. A small amount of yellowish wax is normal, but dark brown wax and unusual or bloody discharge are all abnormal. Dark wax resembling coffee grounds might indicate ear mites, while green or yellow discharge can be a sign of a bad infection. Dogs with yeast infections of the ear often have clear discharge along with very red and inflamed ear tissue. If your dog is rubbing her ear, cries when you touch it, or holds her head cocked to one side, you need to check out the ear. Remember—she does have two, so you have one for comparison if you aren't sure whether something is normal. Many ear infections only affect one ear, most commonly the left.

Sniffing Out Nose Health

The old saying that a healthy dog has a cold nose is true part of the time. Normally a dog's nose feels cooler than the rest of the body and is moist, but on a hot, dry day, your dog's nose will feel warm and dry. If there is discharge coming from the nose, something is not quite right. A purulent, pus-like discharge indicates infection—possibly bacterial or caused by cancer, or a foreign object might be stuck up there. Believe it or not, some dogs even inhale grass, which gets stuck and causes infection! A blood-tinged discharge could indicate trauma, as in your dog hitting his nose on something hard, or could be from cancer or a bleeding disorder. A dog who sneezes frequently can get nosebleeds just as people do.

> **Doggie Dilemmas: What to Do with a Dirty Nose?**
> Don't clean your dog's nose off before heading to the vet. Your vet will want to see the discharge and might need to put some on a slide or culture to see exactly what the problem is and plan the best possible treatment.

Skin Irritation

A dog who's itching, rubbing, and scratching is an uncomfortable dog. Along with the discomfort, the pruritus (itchiness) can be a sign of underlying problems. The skin itself is an important first-line barrier against bacteria and parasites. Skin that is scratched with tiny cuts is ripe ground for infections.

Parasites are the most common cause of itching and scratching. Fleas, ticks, and various mites can all make a dog extremely uncomfortable. These pests might also carry serious, even life-threatening, diseases, which they pass on to their host dog. (See Chapter 12 for more on parasites.)

Allergies are another notorious source of itching. With many dogs, food allergies show up as skin problems rather than stomach or intestinal complaints. Inhaled allergies might stimulate a skin reaction as well.

What to Do

Anything more than an occasional scratch or rub is worth investigating. If your dog is itching and scratching, has open sores or inflamed skin areas, you should contact your veterinarian. Once parasites are ruled out, your veterinarian might do skin tests or blood work to find the cause.

Lethargy, Lameness, and Collapse

This is one of the many reasons why it pays to notice your dog's activity level every day. If your dog normally bounces around, begging someone to throw a toy or go for a walk, you should be concerned if one day he's just resting quietly in the kitchen. Any time your dog holds up a paw, is walking awkwardly, or is reluctant to move, investigate the cause. Lethargy, lameness, and collapse can all be signs of serious problems.

If your dog is very quiet and less active than normal, think over her recent activities. Might be you went for a long, hard romp in the park, or you were at a lake where she swam all day. In that case, she's probably just plain tuckered out—and might be even a little sore. But if you've been spending normal days at home, keep a watch for what's going on. Muscle soreness, a fever, even an upset stomach can all make your dog less active.

Lameness can vary a great deal. A stoic dog might walk despite severe arthritis while a puppy might cry and hold a paw up for minutes after having a toe stepped on. So once again, it's important to know what's normal for your dog.

A dog who actually collapses has a serious problem. It could be heatstroke, internal bleeding, or a heart problem. Cancer, the aftermath of a seizure, or bloat can also cause a dog to collapse suddenly.

What to Do

If your dog's overly lethargic, check gums for pink color (that returns quickly after pressure) to rule out internal bleeding. Check your dog's respiratory rate and heart rate—you can check a pulse on the inside of the thigh if you can't feel the heart itself. If gum color, heart rate, or respiratory rate is abnormal, contact your veterinarian.

As for lameness: If your dog is hobbling on one foot, carefully examine that leg from the toenails on up. A cracked or broken nail can be very painful. Gently feel between toes for any thorns or cuts. Carefully bend each joint as you move up the leg. Even if your dog is tough and doesn't cry or pull away, his breathing will change as you reach the area that hurts. Any redness, unusual swelling, or tender areas should be considered unusual. Your veterinarian will help you decide on appropriate treatment. For minor muscle pulls, a cold soak with the hose for five minutes and an anti-inflammatory prescribed by your veterinarian might do the trick!

Doggie Dilemmas: Could Be a Broken Bone

If your dog won't walk on an injured leg at all, or the lower limb is hanging loosely, you might be dealing with a broken bone. Use extreme care, keep the leg from moving, and get your dog directly to the veterinarian.

In case of collapse, quickly make sure nothing is blocking your dog's airway and head for your veterinarian. If you suspect heatstroke, apply cold compresses to the dog's head and groin while someone else drives.

Swelling or Bloating

A healthy dog normally has a trim figure with a waist that can be clearly seen when you look from above and a tuck-up right before the hind legs when you look from the side. If your dog's figure is round, she might just be overweight, but she could have a medical problem. A sudden increase in width is a definite cause for alarm. Bloat, or gastrointestinal volvulus, is a life-threatening condition that happens when a dog's stomach has twisted. Some owners believe their dog is over-weight when actually the abdomen is distended with fluid. This might be secondary to a heart condition, cancer, or severe inflammation.

Other areas of your dog's body might show swelling as well. Swollen joints can be caused by chronic arthritis or acute infections such as Lyme disease. Cancer might show up as a lump or swelling almost anywhere. These swellings could be benign such as a lipoma or serious such as osteosarcoma, or bone cancer. A bee sting can cause a swollen nose or muzzle.

What to Do

If you're concerned about unusual swelling, ask your veterinarian to check it out.

Remember, bloat is extremely dangerous. If that's what you suspect, your dog needs to go to the veterinarian immediately, even if it's the middle of the night. In the case of fluid, your veterinarian will tap your dog's abdomen and take a fluid sample for analysis and possible culture.

Diarrhea and Vomiting

Vomiting and diarrhea might come together as a pair of gastrointestinal problems, or they might show up separately. These problems can be mild and minor or serious and life-threatening.

The Doggone Truth: Do Dogs Really Eat Grass to Vomit?
It's true—dogs with an upset stomach do sometimes eat grass. But dogs do also graze from time to time for a "salad." Watching what type of grass your dog is chewing will clue you in. Salad-seekers prefer new grass, while a dog with a tummy ache will more likely search out older, tougher grass, which helps more with vomiting.

Diarrhea—when food and fluid pass through your dog's intestinal system faster than normal—can occur after eating unusual foods or from an infection that disrupts the cells lining the intestines. Parasites such as hookworms can also interfere with the normal digestive process and cause diarrhea. A mild case of diarrhea should clear in a day or so.

Diarrhea might smell and look different depending on the cause. For example, puppies with parvo might pass some digested blood, which gives their diarrhea a distinctive odor. A dog with a pancreatic problem that is not digesting fats well might have grayish, smelly diarrhea. Chronic diarrhea (lasting more than a week) can be a sign of a metabolic disease such as pancreatic insufficiency or can be related to cancer.

Dogs might vomit occasionally just from a mild upset stomach. Other than that, some vomiting is triggered in the brain centers where nausea originates. Dogs who get carsick have this type of vomiting—they aren't truly sick, but their bodies aren't happy, either. But most vomiting originates in the gastrointestinal tract—usually the stomach. If your dog eats something bitter or irritating, his body might want to get rid of it, causing him to vomit. Illnesses that disrupt the tract, such as parvo, will also cause vomiting. Vomiting can also occur as part of a generalized problem such as a neuromuscular disease.

What to Do

If your dog vomits once or twice but can keep water down and feels fine otherwise, you can keep an eye on him at home. Holding off on food for a day or so might help your dog recover. He needs fluids, though, so if he can't keep water down, contact your veterinarian. This is even more crucial in puppies and older dogs. After a day with no food, start back with a bland diet and gradually work up to your dog's regular diet. Your veterinarian can provide special prescription bland foods or guide you to homemade substitutes.

Doggie Dilemmas: When Not to Use Vomit-Inducing Medications

Some medications are designed to stimulate vomiting when your dog has eaten a foreign object or something unhealthy such as chocolate or certain poisons. Always check with your veterinarian before making your dog throw up. Some poisons do more damage if they are vomited back up, such as petroleum distillates and certain acids and alkalis.

A dog who is vomiting only or has diarrhea only will be slower to dehydrate than a dog who is dealing with both at the same time.

Along with fluid loss, your dog will lose important electrolytes and minerals that are important for normal body functions. Your veterinarian will be able to help you decide what treatment is necessary and will guide you if he feels home care is all that you need.

No matter how gross the stuff is, save a diarrhea sample for your veterinarian. A fecal sample can help your veterinarian identify parasites, test for diseases such as parvovirus, and check for blood in the stool. A small amount is all that's needed—about a tablespoon at most.

A chronic diarrhea problem can require blood work, special X-rays, and possibly biopsies and endoscopy (examination of the stomach and intestines with a special scope).

Retching without throwing up anything might be a sign of bloat or gastrointestinal volvulus. Bloat is a medical emergency, and if your dog shows the classic symptoms (see Chapter 13), you should head for your veterinarian right away.

A Word about Pain

Whether in humans or animals, pain is a complex phenomenon with physical and psychological components. Short-term or long-term, pain can make your dog's life very unpleasant if it's not managed properly. Pain might certainly have a protective role in minimizing injury and preventing further damage, but unrelieved pain can make a dog's condition worse and has no beneficial effects. Any time you believe your dog is in pain, ask your veterinarian what can be done to help.

Factors that affect each dog's individual response to pain include age, gender, health status, and breed differences. For instance, young dogs have a lower tolerance for sudden pain, but they're less sensitive to the emotional stress or anxiety that accompanies anticipated pain (such as having the anal glands expressed). Healthy dogs tend to tolerate pain better than sick dogs, but sick dogs might be less likely to respond obviously to pain because they don't feel like making the effort. A stoic working or herding breed might show less response to pain than an excitable or sensitive breed.

The response to pain can be involuntary or voluntary. For instance, when a groomer's nail clippers cut into the quick, the painfully sensitive blood vessel that feeds the nail, the dog reflexively jerks his paw back. That's an involuntary response. A voluntary response is based on experience. A dog who's had his nails clipped too short in the past remembers the pain and jerks his paw back before the clippers even touch the nail.

Recognizing Signs of Pain

Pain is often difficult to recognize and interpret in dogs. When humans are in pain, they usually don't hesitate to let others know about it. But dogs are a bit subtler—most try to hide pain. It's an evolutionary response dictated by thousands of years of predatory knowledge: The weak don't survive. (Or maybe dogs secretly pass it on that pain means

is your dog ill?

a trip to the vet.) While they're generally not as secretive as cats, dogs will make a pretty good effort to keep you from knowing they're not in tip-top condition. You have to be alert and observant to figure out that your dog isn't feeling his best.

The early signs of pain are subtle. They might include eating less, failing to greet you at the door when you come home from work, or not wanting to be groomed when a dog normally enjoys that. More obvious signs of pain include limping, reluctance to move, squinting or pawing at the eyes, crying out or whining when touched, or even snapping when touched. Any unexplained abnormality in your dog's routine behavior or activity level is significant and warrants a visit to the veterinarian. Common signs of pain you should watch for include the following:

- Changes in personality or attitude, such as a normally quiet and docile dog becoming aggressive or an aggressive dog becoming quiet
- Abnormal vocalizations, such as whining or whimpering, especially when a painful area is touched or the dog is forced to move
- Licking, biting, scratching, or shaking of one area
- Piloerection, a reflex of the muscles at the base of the hair shafts that causes the hair to stand on end
- Changes in posture or movement, such as limping, holding a paw up, or tensing the abdominal and back muscles to produce a tucked-up appearance

- Changes in activity level, including restlessness, pacing, lethargy, or reluctance to move
- Loss of appetite
- Changes in facial expression, such as dull eyes or pinned ears
- Changes in bowel movements or urination, such as straining

Your veterinarian will check your dog's heart rate, respiratory rate, and body temperature. All of these tend to increase in the presence of pain. The veterinarian might also check a blood sample for elevations in glucose, corticosteroid, and catecholamine concentrations.

Diagnosing Pain

To find the source of pain, your veterinarian will probably begin by palpating your dog's body, examining it by hand to check the condition of the organs and search for painful lumps or bumps. He might put pressure on the trigger points along the spine and check the range of motion of the legs. Once he knows where the pain is, your vet can try to figure out what's causing it and how to treat it.

When there isn't an obvious cause for pain, sophisticated diagnostic techniques can help. These include analysis of the cerebrospinal fluid, radiographs of the spine using dye (myelography), measurements of the electrical activity in the muscles (electromyography), and brain imaging with computed tomography (CT) or magnetic resonance imaging (MRI) scans.

is your dog ill?

171

Types of Pain

Pain comes in a variety of forms, and each type can be treated differently. Here's a brief overview.

Acute Pain

Often described as short-term pain or pain with an easily identifiable cause, acute pain is the body's way to warn of injury or disease. It usually starts out as a sudden, sharp pain that becomes an ache. Acute pain begins in a specific area and might then spread out. It can be mild or severe and might last for only a few days or for weeks, depending on the type of injury or disease. Pain is most intense within the first twenty-four to seventy-two hours of injury.

Veterinarians commonly treat acute pain that is the result of either trauma or surgery. Causes include fractures, bowel obstructions, bladder stones, and gastroenteritis (stomachache). Depending on the cause, acute pain responds well to medication such as analgesic drugs (pain relievers). It can also be relieved surgically.

Chronic Pain

Chronic pain is pain that lasts for six months or longer. Chronic pain is often associated with a disease that has a long duration, such as cancer. This debilitating type of pain requires long-term specialized treatment. Unfortunately, chronic pain is more difficult to treat than acute pain. To deal with it effectively, your veterinarian might need to perform a number of diagnostic tests and try many different approaches to pain relief.

Surgical Pain

Pain resulting from surgery is one of the most obvious forms of acute pain. Surgery (and some invasive diagnostic procedures) can cause significant pain in dogs, but because dogs can't communicate their level of discomfort, it's difficult to provide proper pain medication. If dogs don't get the necessary pain relief, they can lose their appetite and become stressed, both of which reduce the effectiveness of the surgery.

Veterinarians have learned that the best way to prevent surgical pain is to provide presurgical pain relief. Anesthesia blocks the knowledge of pain during surgery, but now veterinarians can give dogs a combination of pain-relief and anesthetic drugs. Presurgical pain relief means less anesthesia can be used, as well as less postsurgical pain relief. The improved safety of anesthetic drugs, combined with this ability to provide presurgical pain relief, also allows surgeons to perform more invasive procedures than they could in the past.

Good surgical techniques can also reduce pain from surgery. These include minimizing tissue trauma by making smaller incisions and preventing tension on suture lines. Bandages to pad and protect the traumatized area are also essential. After surgery, making the dog comfortable on warm bedding as he comes out of the anesthetic haze can also help.

Postsurgical Pain

Many advances have been made in pain relief for animals, but managing postsurgical and chronic pain is still difficult. That's because not all drugs are effective in every situation. Some cause side effects when used over a long period, and some aren't convenient for owners to give at home. Researchers have hope, however, that a new slow-release narcotic drug will be able to provide convenient, safe, and long-lasting pain relief for dogs and improve the treatment of chronic and postsurgical pain. Currently, no medications are licensed for use in dogs to treat postoperative pain, although some veterinarians, with the informed consent of the dog's owner, might choose to use certain medications to help the dog feel more comfortable after surgery.

Managing Pain

The first thing to realize is that complete elimination of pain isn't necessarily possible or desirable. The main goal is to help your dog cope with pain so he doesn't suffer. Successful pain management allows a dog to continue to engage in normal activities, such as eating, sleeping, moving around, and interacting with people or other animals.

Medication

Most veterinarians use drugs with pain-relieving properties as the first line of defense. Opioids, for instance, usually have the effects of dulling the senses, relieving pain, or inducing sleep. Opioid patches

the "i have a life" dog owner's guide

placed on a dog's skin can provide long-lasting and steady pain relief, unlike shorter-acting medications that can wear off before the next dose is given.

 The Doggone Truth: Toxic Drugs

Dogs process drugs differently than people. Never give your dog any kind of pain-relief medication without first checking with your veterinarian. Tylenol and ibuprofen, for example, are toxic to dogs even in very small amounts.

Some analgesic drugs include local anesthetics, which numb only a particular area. Certain medications known as nonsteroidal anti-inflammatory drugs (NSAIDs) are often used to treat the chronic pain of arthritis or cancer. NSAIDs don't directly eliminate pain, but they can decrease it by treating inflammation. Several NSAIDs have been developed specifically for use in dogs, including carprofen, etodolac, meloxicam, and deracoxib.

Different types of drugs have a sedative effect. They work to decrease anxiety and can enhance the effectiveness of analgesic drugs, but they don't necessarily relieve pain in and of themselves.

The dose and effect duration of analgesic drugs varies greatly from dog to dog. Your veterinarian might also choose to use a combination of analgesic drugs from different drug classes to achieve the best pain relief and reduce the risk of side effects. As your dog's needs change, your veterinarian might modify the dose or frequency of administration. He might also require periodic blood work to make sure the drug isn't affecting liver function, which is a common side effect.

More Than Just Medicine

Effective pain management goes beyond drugs. Keeping your dog comfortable will also help him feel better more quickly. If he's recovering at home, place his bed in a quiet, well-ventilated area. Take steps to limit his stress, and keep visits short and low-key. Diet is important too. When your dog's in pain he might not feel like eating, but he needs nutrition to heal. Tempt your dog's appetite with canned food. If that doesn't work, try warming his food in the microwave. The heat will improve his ability to smell the food, which should help his appetite. Test it with your finger before giving it to him to make sure there aren't any hot spots.

Weight loss can help relieve your dog's pain, especially if he suffers from an orthopedic condition such as arthritis or hip dysplasia. Veterinarians now believe that overweight dogs with painful hips and lameness caused by osteoarthritis might improve through weight-reduction alone. While there's no cure for osteoarthritis or hip dysplasia, a weight-reduction plan might delay the need for surgery. This is especially important for large-breed dogs, whose size puts more stress on the joints, or active dogs such as sporting breeds, who enjoy lots of running or hunting.

Alternative Therapies

These therapies are no longer unusual for animals; many traditionally trained veterinarians now offer their clients a full range of services by joining forces with or making referrals to practitioners that offer these treatments. Among the therapies that might benefit dogs are acupuncture, chiropractic therapy, magnetic field therapy, massage, and nutraceuticals.

 The Doggone Truth: Last Resort

Steroids can be used for pain relief, but they're a last resort. Long term, steroids have a detrimental effect on the health of joint tissues, particularly cartilage. Long-term use of steroids can lead to diabetes and adrenal gland problems.

Few studies have been done to prove the effectiveness of these treatments. Much of what's known has been extrapolated from studies in humans. Nonetheless, many dog owners believe alternative therapies have made a difference in their pets' quality of life. Because not much is known about how or why certain treatments or techniques work in animals, always go to an experienced practitioner to ensure safety.

is your dog ill?

Chapter 12

Parasite Problems

 PARASITES ARE NASTY little creatures that can only exist through living off another being—in some cases, your poor pooch. Internal and external pests such as worms, ticks, and fleas drain nutrients from dogs, cause a wide variety of health problems, and can even transmit diseases. Your mission is to keep your dog as parasite-free as possible for a long, healthy life.

My Dog Has Fleas

Fleas are active devils. They leap many times their own height and run swiftly. They've also become resistant to many anti-flea medications. They make healthy dogs itch, can stimulate severe allergic reactions, and can also carry other parasites and diseases. Tapeworms can be transmitted by fleabites. Life-threatening problems such as bubonic plague (not common, but seen in the Southwest) and a certain type of typhus can also be transmitted through fleabites.

A heavy load of fleas on a small puppy can cause serious anemia. Fleas will even make a meal of your blood if they get the chance, along with any other furry pets such as rabbits and cats. Dealing with fleas is like planning to fight a war!

Where Do They Come From?

Fleas live for short periods of time on the ground or in houses, though they must be on their hosts to feed and breed. Most of the fleas we see on our dogs are actually the cat flea—*Ctenocephalides felis*. Once adult fleas find a suitable host, they feed by taking blood meals. Then the females lay eggs, which may stick to your dog's hair or fall off in the areas where he sleeps, lies, or walks in your house. Larvae hatch and go into a pupa where the adult fleas will develop.

Canine Quick Fix: A Fast Way to Check for Fleas

Part your dog's hair and look for tiny running bodies. It might be easiest to roll him over and look in the relatively hairless area of the groin. If you see or feel dark grit in your dog's coat, take some off and put it on a white paper towel. Add a drop of water. If the grit dissolves and turns red, you know it's flea feces—the red is from the blood meals.

Winning the War

Fighting fleas calls for a concerted effort. All your pets need to be treated—even those who don't show signs of itching. You need to get rid of the adult fleas, stop reproduction, and prevent new fleas from joining the family.

When you're treating fleas, remember that a flea bath will only get rid of the eggs and adult fleas on your pet at that moment. Once he jumps out of the tub all clean and flea-free, new fleas will immediately jump on from the carpet or ground. You need to follow up the bath with a dip, spray, powder, collar, or topical treatment to deter or kill fleas if they try to jump on your dog. Your rugs need to be thoroughly cleaned, and don't forget areas along walls and behind doors. You can also set off "flea bombs" to catch any fleas that are left. Outside, try planting chrysanthemums, spreading borax or diatomaceous earth, and discouraging rodents (who could serve as hosts) from living near your home.

Keep Those Fleas at Bay

Preventing flea infestations is easier than getting rid of them once they've moved in. Take action before you see evidence. When warm weather approaches, start thinking about flea control (often combined with tick control). There are new medications that act as flea birth control, and insect growth regulators stop any fleas that get on your dog from successfully reproducing. Finally, you can also find drugs that act to kill fleas. Many of these medications now come in topical forms that can be applied to your dog once monthly. Pyrethrins (from chrysanthemums) are found in many flea-control products.

Tick Tactics

These tough arachnids not only eat blood meals, they can also carry many serious, life-threatening diseases. They come in a variety of sizes (all small, though), and the primary species vary from region to region. Ticks can be differentiated from fleas in that they are rounder and they either walk or are firmly fixed to your dog's body. Most are brown, but some, such as deer ticks, are very small and whitish in color. Female ticks get very large after a blood meal and their color changes from brown to grayish.

A Tick's Life

The ticks most often found on dogs are the dog ticks, Dermacenter and Rhipicephalus, and the deer tick Ixodes. These ticks go through four life stages. Female ticks lay eggs after they engorge with a blood meal. The eggs are deposited in cracks and crevices or on the ground. The eggs hatch into larvae that climb up on grass, hitch a ride on a

parasite problems

host, and take a big blood meal themselves. The next stage is a nymph and then another cycle of hitching a ride on a host, a blood meal, and on to the next stage—the adult.

Disease Carriers

Unfortunately, ticks aren't only a threat for the blood-sucking damage they can do. Many ticks can carry dangerous diseases such as Lyme disease, canine ehrlichiosis and babesiosis, even Rocky Mountain spotted fever (which isn't confined to the Rocky Mountain area anymore). These diseases might show up as problems in the blood with immunity deficits or anemia; swollen, painful joints; rashes; fevers; and damage to the heart. These sidekicks have the potential to kill your dog. You are susceptible to many of these diseases as well, if a tick feeds off you.

Prepare Your Battle Plans

Like fighting fleas, fighting ticks is a two-stage battle—removal and prevention. If you find ticks on your dog, they need to be carefully removed. There are special tweezers made to remove them, and you should wear gloves to prevent infection. Do not use a lighted match or pour gasoline on the tick. It doesn't work and is dangerous to your dog. If the head is left in your dog's skin, a localized infection could result. Your veterinarian can help you treat those spots.

Many topical agents and collars used for flea control also work against ticks. You want something that will kill the ticks almost immediately—they must feed for twenty-four to forty-eight hours to pass on most diseases. Better yet, some products will repel them from your dog to begin with. If you live in an area with ticks or plan to travel where ticks are common, discuss the best and safest protection methods with your veterinarian.

Managing Mites and Lice

Mites are small parasites and three main types can be found on dogs: the ear mite, Otodectes; the sarcoptic mange mite, Sarcoptes; and the demodectic or red mange mite, Demodex. Skin problems caused by mites are often referred to as mange. Demodex is not contagious, though ear mites and sarcoptic mites are. They will spread among dogs, from cats to dogs, and (rarely) even to people! If one pet in your household has mites, check all pets carefully. Lice also attack dogs via their skin, though they aren't very common in dogs.

Ear Mites

Ear mites sometimes occur in dogs who live with cats. You might notice dark, coffee-ground type buildup in your dog's ears, and she might be scratching a bit. Your veterinarian can diagnose a mite infestation by examining a swab of the discharge under a microscope. Most cases can be treated with topical ear medications, though severe cases might need a parasiticide.

Sarcoptic Mange

A dog with sarcoptic mange is usually very unhappy and uncomfortable. These mites burrow into the top layers of the skin, where even a few of them can cause plenty of itching. Dogs with sarcoptic mange can barely walk, they stop to scratch so much. With all the scratching, they have open skin areas, which are then in danger of infection. Sarcoptic mange mites are contagious, and dogs with these parasites often have picked them up from local wildlife, including foxes and squirrels.

Diagnosing sarcoptic mange can be tricky. Skin scrapes are the best method, but it can be hard to find mites. If your veterinarian suspects sarcoptic mange, he might start treatment even with a negative skin scrape.

Sarcoptic mange is often treated with a combination of drugs and with baths or dips. Any related infections must also be treated, and your veterinarian will try to make your dog comfortable and relieve some of the itching.

Demodex—Mite of the Red Mange

Demodex is a tiny mite that can be found in normal dogs. Most dogs get along quite well with their demodectic mites and have no

the "i have a life" dog owner's guide

problems. Unfortunately, some dogs have immune problems, and in these dogs, the mites overgrow and cause skin reactions. A few red spots on a puppy can be treated topically or might clear by themselves with no treatment. Dogs who have more than five spots or large areas of reddened, sore skin have generalized Demodex. This is a marker for immune problems.

Demodex is usually easily diagnosed by a skin scraping. Dogs with generalized Demodex will need serious treatment, often with both drugs and dips combined. Since this condition is associated with a genetic defect, dogs who suffer from it should be spayed or neutered and not bred.

Cheyletiella—Walking Dandruff

Cheyletiella is a short-lived mite most often seen on puppies. It shows up as a line of dandruff down their backs. This mite is not usually a serious threat to your dog's health and can be treated with medicated baths.

Lice

Lice come in two main types—biting and sucking. Biting lice tend to be smaller and can move quickly. Neither type is very common in dogs. Lice are usually host-specific, which means they rarely move from people to dogs or vice versa. Puppies sometimes have lice because of a dirty environment. A large number of lice could make a puppy anemic, but normally the effects are just poor coats and nits or eggs attached to hair shafts. In most cases, medicated baths or dips will take care of this parasite.

Common Internal Parasites

The most common internal parasites in dogs are roundworms (especially the Toxocara species), hookworms (primarily Ancylostoma), and whipworms (Oxyuris). Reports suggest that more than 80 percent of all puppies will be born with, or quickly acquire, roundworms. These parasites live in the intestines and drain vital nutrients that growing puppies need. On rare occasions a puppy will vomit up roundworms, but worms are normally diagnosed when your veterinarian checks a fecal sample. Whipworms do not pass as many eggs as roundworms or hookworms, so repeated fecal checks might be necessary. Your veterinarian might treat for them anyway based on clinical signs. Picking up after your dog is very important to reduce the chances of internal parasites being spread.

Roundworms

Roundworms can infect puppies before they are born and can also be transmitted via the dam's milk. Adult dogs get roundworms by accidentally ingesting eggs deposited on the ground. The immature larvae migrate through your dog's body and can cause damage to the liver and lungs. Puppies with roundworms often have a bloated abdomen, dull coat, diarrhea, and possibly intestinal blockages. Adult dogs develop some resistance, but even they can show the effects of roundworms.

 FIDO **The Doggone Truth: Check for Worms**

All puppies should be checked for roundworms and dewormed. These parasites can also infect people. While they don't reproduce in humans, they can cause serious damage, even blindness, while migrating through tissues. Young children who play in dirt are at greatest risk.

Hookworms

Hookworms are smaller than roundworms but with a set of mouth hooks that dig into the intestines and drain nutrients and blood. Again, puppies can be infected in utero or via their dam's milk. Hookworms can be ingested and can also penetrate the skin, and they cause skin lesions in people as they migrate through the body. Because of their voracious nature, hookworms can actually kill a puppy by causing severe anemia. Dogs with hookworms will show anemia, possibly bloody diarrhea, weight loss, and poor coats.

Whipworms

Luckily, whipworms are not as prevalent as roundworms or hookworms. These are small intestinal parasites with a whiplike, tapering tail (hence the name). The eggs need to be ingested to complete their life cycle, but they can survive in the ground for long periods of time. Whipworms cause diarrhea, often with mucus and blood. Dogs with whipworms might defecate frequently and strain to do so. A large number of whipworms can be a serious drain on an adult dog, let alone a puppy. Whipworms are resistant to treatment, so repeated treatments might be necessary. It is also important to clean up the environment, or your dog can easily become reinfected. Cement runs can be bleached; dig up dirt runs and replace with fresh soil.

Tapeworms

Tapeworms are more often discovered at home, when segments are passed out of the anus, than by fecal checks. There are two common species of tapeworms found in dogs and a few unusual ones.

The Usual Suspects

The most common tapeworms are *Dipylidium caninum* and *Taenia pisiformis*. These two tapeworms have different life cycles, and differentiating them is important for treating your dog and preventing future infestation. Dipylidium use fleas as their intermediate host. Dogs who have fleas often accidentally eat one while grooming and scratching. Taenia use rodents as their intermediate host, and dogs who hunt mice or rabbits can pick them up while hunting if they eat their prey. Keep your dog flea-free and minimize hunting opportunities if you want to avoid tapeworms.

The Doggone Truth: Less-Common Pests

Some parasites, such as lungworms and flukes, are not commonly found in dogs but can still cause serious health problems. Some have geographical limitations, and others require certain hosts. While small in numbers, their effects can be big, so check with your vet to find out if any of these more unusual parasites are indigenous to your area.

Protozoan Problems

Protozoal parasites are small single-cell organisms that can't exist well outside their given host or a specialized environment. Many can also affect people. Good hygiene is very important in dealing with these and any parasites.

The best way to diagnose protozoal infections is with a fresh fecal sample. In this case, your veterinarian will take a small sample directly from your dog's rectum. The sample will be mixed with saline and examined under a microscope for protozoa actively moving around. A regular fecal test would kill the protozoa and make them virtually impossible to detect.

Giardia

This protozoal parasite is hardy and can exist for long periods of time in a wet environment. Streams and ponds are its favorite sites. Drinking infected water can lead to severe diarrhea, sometimes with blood or mucus. The cysts are then passed into the feces and can contaminate other bodies of water. There are treatments for Giardia, but it can be difficult to diagnose. Your veterinarian might need to check multiple fecal samples, including some fresh ones taken on a rectal exam. This parasite can be spread to people as well, so you and your dog should both avoid drinking water from streams or ponds in areas where this parasite is known to exist. There is now a vaccine for dogs in epidemic areas.

Coccidia

Dogs who live in a less-than-clean environment, especially puppies, can ingest coccidian cysts through contaminated food or fecal material. Dogs with Coccidia might have diarrhea, sometimes with blood. In puppies this can be a debilitating disease. People are resistant, but kennel areas still need to be kept immaculately clean to prevent puppies picking up these protozoa. Diagnosis is fairly easy with fecal checks.

Treating Intestinal Parasites

As always, one of the best treatments for disease problems is prevention. Keeping your dog's play area clean, picking up after your dog on walks, yearly or even twice-yearly fecal checks, and helping your dog to stay in the best condition possible all reduce parasite problems or at least keep them to a minimum. Still, don't feel like you've done something wrong if your dog gets a parasite. Even the best-cared-for dogs can pick them up just by walking where another dog deposited eggs days before.

If your dog does pick up some intestinal parasites, there are many safe medications that will kill the pests, including pyrantel pamoate, ivermectin, and febendazole. If you see worms or suspect a parasite problem, check with your veterinarian. Many over-the-counter dewormers are not effective. Certain parasites, such as whipworms, might require repeated treatments on a set schedule. If so, do a follow-up fecal check after finishing a course of treatment to be sure it was effective.

Canine Quick Fix: Double Duty
Some heartworm and flea and tick preventives also guard against selected intestinal parasites. Check with your veterinarian to see if one of these makes sense for your dog.

Nontraditional Treatments
There are some herbal and homeopathic medications believed to be effective for dewormings. Remember, just because something is natural or organic does not mean it's safe! Consult your veterinarian first. Black walnut and garlic are often touted for dewormings, but if used incorrectly these could be toxic to your dog. (The same goes for many traditional dewormers if used incorrectly.)

Heartworm

This is a big one for dogs. Heartworms, *Dirofilaria immitus*, are potentially life-threatening parasites. Originally seen only in the Deep South and isolated pockets around the country, heartworm has now spread to most of the United States. It is spread by many types of mosquitoes and is a threat all year round in warm areas.

Adult heartworms live and thrive in dogs' hearts and pulmonary arteries. Some might also be in the lungs in large blood vessels. Heartworms live a long life—sometimes as long as five years! During this time, if there are both males and females present, they produce many tiny young, called microfilaria. The microfilaria get into the bloodstream and are picked up when a mosquito bites your dog. These microfilaria develop in the mosquito and then move to its mouth so that they can be injected into another dog when the mosquito feeds.

Dogs with a mild case of heartworm will cough, lose some of their stamina, and might be weak or short of breath. The worms block the blood supply of fresh oxygen to other tissues, including the lungs, heart, kidneys, and liver. By the time these clinical signs show up, some of the damage is irreparable. Dogs can die from a heavy load of heartworms.

Pinning It Down

Heartworm diagnosis can involve multiple specialized tests. There are a few simple and easy tests your veterinarian can run right in the clinic. The first is to check a blood sample for antigens. This test picks up protein in the blood shed by adult heartworms. It can pick up infections early—with luck before the adults are even reproducing. A second test screens a blood sample for actual microfilaria. While microfilaria found in blood samples are almost always from heartworms, they do need to be clearly identified before any treatment is started.

Your veterinarian might also want to do X-rays or even an echocardiogram (special ultrasound of the heart) to look for worms or the damage they cause. Enlargement of the heart and the large blood vessels that go to the lungs are highly suggestive of heartworm infection. A complete blood panel might be done before any treatment is started to see if your dog already has liver or kidney damage.

Good Riddance to Worms

There are numerous preventive medications for heartworm, ranging from daily pills to monthly medications. Work is also being done on even longer-range products. Some medications require that your dog tests negative for heartworm first, as a rapid die-off of the parasites could cause shock reactions. Some of these products can be effective against some of the intestinal parasites your dog is susceptible to as well. Some breeds are sensitive to ivermectin, a common ingredient in heartworm preventives, and should use other medications.

Dogs who are diagnosed with heartworm infections will need treatments to kill both the adults and the microfilaria. Currently the only approved treatment for the adults is an organic arsenic compound—obviously a drug to be used with care, as you want to poison the worms but not your dog! This medication requires intravenous administration and your dog might need to be hospitalized for care and observation. Dogs must be kept quiet after this treatment. While the adult heartworms are now dead, your dog's body must absorb the remains and keep any pieces from shedding off and causing trouble. Some veterinarians have been successful using ivermectin at higher than preventive dosages as well.

Chapter 13

First Aid for Your Furry Friend

 AS A POOCH PARENT, you've got to be ready to nurse a few bumps, scrapes, and other minor injuries here and there. There might also be occasions when you need to handle more serious situations. Although serious injuries require quick medical attention, there are a number of things you can to do help your dog in cases of lesser accidents. Whatever the injury, remember: Never panic! If you panic, you won't be thinking clearly, and your dog will pick up on your tension. Stay calm, and you can help your pal with first aid predicaments.

Your Canine First-Aid Kit

Before we get into injury specifics, let's take care of some basics. A good first aid-kit for your dog is a must. People need most of these things, too, so you'll be covering all of your bases. (With any of the medications listed below, always check first with your veterinarian and/or the National Animal Poison Control Center about proper dosage.) A good dog first-aid kit should include the following items:

- 🐾 **Activated charcoal:** This is to be used in some poisoning cases.
- 🐾 **Antihistamine:** Keep an antihistamine, such as Benadryl, on hand to use after insect stings or other mild allergic reactions.
- 🐾 **Artificial tears:** These are useful for flushing dust or seeds out of your dog's eyes.
- 🐾 **Bandage material:** This could include gauze rolls, gauze pads, and Telfa pads to cover wounds.
- 🐾 **Diarrhea medication:** This can be as simple as Pepto-Bismol tablets or Kaopectate.
- 🐾 **Disposable hot and cold packs:** These are handy for applying to sore areas.
- 🐾 **Hydrogen peroxide:** This is an extremely effective way to make your dog vomit. Do not give this until you check with your veterinarian or NAPCC to see if this is the correct treatment!
- 🐾 **Ointments:** Tubes of antibiotic, corticosteroid, and aloe ointments are good for small wounds, cuts, and sores.
- 🐾 **Pain medications:** Ask your veterinarian for some nonsteroidal pain medications to have on hand for emergencies.
- 🐾 **Saline:** A small bottle of saline to flush out sore ears or wounds is helpful.
- 🐾 **Scissors:** These make life easier if you have to cut bandages or gauze.
- 🐾 **Silver nitrate or styptic pencil:** These help to stop minor bleeding, such as when a toenail gets trimmed into the quick.

- 🐾 **Tape:** Pack some adhesive tape for fastening bandages (leave a tab for quick removal!) and some duct tape to put over cut pads as a temporary bootie if you are hiking. Vetwrap or Elastikon are useful for keeping bandages on—just don't make them too tight!
- 🐾 **Thermometer:** Rectal ones are the most accurate, but there are also ear and digital models for dogs.
- 🐾 **Tweezers:** These are good for removing splinters and thorns. Some are specialized for removing ticks as well.

For the "natural pet," you might want to include Rescue Remedy for stress and trauma, arnica for trauma and wounds (use only the homeopathic version and give orally), plus a sterile needle for the acupuncture point under the nose that stimulates breathing. (Ask a veterinary acupuncturist to show you where this point is and teach you how to use the needle.) If your pet has special conditions, such as epilepsy or severe reactions to bee stings, ask your veterinarian about diazepam pills or enemas for seizures and an EpiPen kit for anaphylaxis.

Canine CPR

CPR (Cardiopulmonary Resuscitation) stimulates the heart and lungs to function. Remembering the basics of CPR is as easy as ABC: A for airway, B for breath, and C for circulation. Any pet owner can learn these emergency basics.

Some Red Cross groups now offer CPR classes with a special practice dog. Many of them hold pet first-aid classes too. These classes are well worth your time. Check with your local Red Cross. Ask your veterinarian about pet CPR and first-aid courses, too.

How to Do It

Drowning, choking, electric shocks, or trauma can cause your dog to stop breathing or his heart to stop beating. If you have such an emergency, first you need to have a clear airway. Close the muzzle and breathe into the nose. Try five or six quick breaths right away. If that doesn't work, you need to go into a routine of about fifteen or twenty breaths per minute. You should be able to see the chest wall expand as you breathe into the dog's nose.

To get circulation going, your dog will need chest compressions. Place her gently on her right side on a reasonably flat surface. Make sure there are no broken ribs you would be pushing on. (If ribs are broken, your dog's chest will move in an erratic pattern.) For a big dog, put the heel of your hand against the chest, above and behind the dog's elbow, then put your other hand on top of the first. A small dog or puppy might just need one hand around the chest. Push quickly ten times. If you don't get any response, you need to do sixty to eighty compressions a minute.

If you have a partner, one of you can breathe into the nose while the other person does chest compressions. If you have to work alone, alternate breathing and chest compressions.

Poisonous Plants and Other Toxins

All household toxins should be shut away in cabinets out of your dog's reach. You can use locks or childproof catches. Better yet, put them in a cabinet in the basement or garage behind a closed door. The more barriers between your dog and the toxin, the better! Never repackage products. If your dog accidentally ingests something, you need to be able to read the ingredients label to the Poison Control Center to know what actions to take.

Canine Quick Fixes: Stay Safe by Restraining Your Dog

If your dog is frightened and hurt, you need a restraint, such as a muzzle, to keep both of you safe. Practice with one when you are not in crisis—to accustom your dog to the muzzle and to make sure it fits. In a pinch, you can also take a strip of gauze, loop it around your dog's nose, cross it under the chin, and tie it behind the ears. (The bony tissue on top of the nose means you don't have to worry about shutting off airways.)

There are many common plants including azaleas, poinsettias, and daffodils that are toxic to dogs. Unfortunately some dogs, especially puppies, like to chew on plants. And they don't discriminate between the caustic lily and the safe spider plant. Even if your houseplants are all safe, odds are at least some of the trees, shrubs, or flowers in your yard are mildly poisonous. It pays to walk around your yard with a field guide and identify all the plants you find.

What to Do

Quite simply, be aware of poisonous substances, and keep them away from your dog—it's just not worth risking his health. Separate large toxic shrubs and trees from your dog. You could fence in a safe part of the yard for your dog to play in, or put small individual fences around the plants that might cause problems. Remember that fruits of certain trees, like chokecherries, can be poisonous. Pick up any fruits like these, as well as any rotting fruit that might attract bees along with your hungry hound!

Also be very careful of any mushrooms that sprout up in your yard. If you find your dog chewing on one, grab a similar one for identification right away and be prepared to drive to your veterinarian. The same advice goes for any chewed-up plant.

FIDO The Doggone Truth: Less-Conspicuous Toxins

Not all substances that are dangerous to dogs come with a skull and crossbones plastered on the label. Chocolate, especially dark baking chocolate, can be toxic to dogs, as can coffee, grapes, and alcohol. The same is true for many supplements. Even those labeled as "natural" or "organic" might be toxic to dogs.

If your dog ever gets into a chemical substance that you think might be toxic, immediately call your veterinarian or emergency clinic. Have the container of the substance handy to read them the ingredients and to be able to guesstimate how much your dog might have consumed. Have your first-aid kit at hand, and use it as directed.

Know the number for your local poison control center, or, even better, call directly to the National Animal Poison Control Center, at 1-888-4ANIHELP (426-4435) or 1-900-443-0000.

Small Cuts

Small cuts that don't leave gaping wounds can often be treated at home. Flush the wound gently with saline solution, water, or a chlorhexidine wash. Tamed iodine solutions (like Betadine) can be used to clean small cuts as well. The antibacterial properties of iodine and chlorhexidine can help to prevent infections. In general, small wounds will heal fine if left open and kept clean. Apply a small amount of antibiotic ointment to help keep the tissues moist. A gaping opening might need sutures to keep the tissues underneath hydrated and healthy.

Punctures and Large Wounds

Punctures are dangerous wounds. What you see on the surface might not give you an accurate idea of the damage to tissues underneath. Bleeding could be occurring inside and muscles might be ripped. These wounds tend to close over and allow bacteria to flourish inside. A puncture wound could need daily flushing to keep it open, prevent infections, and to encourage it to heal from the inside out. Large wounds might need suturing or daily wound care, including alternating wet and dry bandages to encourage healing and minimize the chances of infection. Your veterinarian can instruct you in the care needed for these types of injuries and might prescribe antibiotics.

Doggie Dilemmas: Cut Arteries

A wound spraying blood usually means a cut artery. Apply pressure directly to the area. If the bleeding stops quickly, observe the wound for the next hour. Only small arteries will stop quickly with pressure. If bleeding starts again, your dog might need veterinary attention.

Nail Injuries

Most dog parents will face a broken or bleeding toenail at some point. You might accidentally cut too close to the quick while trimming your dog's nails. Or your dog might catch and tear a toenail on her own. Either way, it's very painful.

If your dog has totally torn the nail off a toe, there is usually very little bleeding. The foot is very painful, and the sensitive red tissue is easy to see. A nail that is cracked but not totally torn off might be even more painful as your dog will push the broken edge into sensitive areas with every step. It makes sense to remove that remaining bit of nail, so a trip to your veterinarian is a good idea. The sensitive tissues underneath will toughen up, and the nail will grow back, but your dog's foot could be sore for a week or more. Try to avoid walking on rough surfaces with your dog during that time.

What to Do

The most important thing to do for a bleeding nail is to stop the bleeding so that clotting can occur. The best way is to hold a silver nitrate stick on the area. This will sting, so you might need help holding your dog. If you don't have silver nitrate, there are other ways to stop the bleeding. Some people swear by sticking the offending toe into a bar of soap or a bowl of corn meal. Keep your dog quiet and don't let him lick the foot until blood has clotted.

Running Wild

For most dogs, a run-in with local wildlife typically means a brisk chase after a rabbit or squirrel. Sometimes the encounters get more intense, though. Always keep your dog up-to-date on rabies vaccinations. Saliva from a wild animal, in bites or even on the coat, can carry this deadly virus.

Skunked!

If your dog gets sprayed, don't reach for the tomato juice (to be at all effective, you need to do multiple rinses). First, make sure your dog's eyes are okay. The spray from a scared skunk can be quite painful if it gets in the eyes. Flush your dog's eyes with artificial tears. Then you're ready to move on to cleanup. There are some effective commercial preparations you can get at the local pet store, or you can try this excellent home recipe. Wear rubber gloves, and keep the mixture out of your eyes and your dog's.

1. In a bucket or other open container, combine 1 quart hydrogen peroxide, ¼ cup baking soda, and 1 tsp. liquid dish soap.
2. Sponge the mixture over your dog, working it into the coat.
3. Leave this on for 3 to 5 minutes, then rinse.

A Prickly Situation

Encounters with porcupines can be more serious. A curious dog who sticks his nose a bit too close might turn away with a mouth and nose full of quills! These quills have tiny scales at the sharp ends, which makes them difficult to pull out. If your dog is lucky enough to have only three or four, you might try to pull them yourself with a pair of pliers and a helper. Do not trim the ends of the quills; that only makes it more difficult to pull them out.

A dog with quills inside the mouth or more than just a couple will need a trip to the veterinarian, some sedation, and careful removal. Quills left behind (including those your dog might have chewed off to the skin level) can migrate into your dog's tissues and cause abscesses.

Your veterinarian might give you antibiotics for your dog to prevent any infections.

Dog Fight

Keep your dog on leash unless you are in a very safe area and only dogs you know are around, because it's best to avoid dog fights from the start. With your dog on leash you can quickly pull her to you, scare off another dog, or even pick your dog up if you have to. Many aggressive dogs will back off at the united front of a dog and her person.

If a fight does break out, do not reach in to grab your dog. Start in with the water works—douse your dog with a hose or bucket. That usually startles the dogs enough to stop the fight. Swishing a broom or rake between combatants might work, or making a loud noise—even a whistle—can be a distraction.

What to Do

Once you get your dog away from a fight, check his coat. Be sure to part the hair carefully to check for any bruises or bite wounds down in the skin. A puncture wound might look minor on the surface, but there could be muscle damage underneath.

If your dog is bleeding heavily, put pressure on the area and get to your veterinarian quickly. If your dog has open cuts, you need to clean them carefully and call your veterinarian. As bacteria would be moving from one dog's mouth to another dog's body, the chance of infection is high. Your dog could need antibiotics.

When Your Buddy Gets Burned

Having a burn injury is extremely painful, whether it's from a paw accidentally hitting a burner when jumping up, or running through the embers of a bonfire. Burns can be quite serious, depending on how deep they go. You can help healing with some quick first aid.

What to Do

Despite the old tales recommending putting butter or other greasy substances on burns, we now know better. The grease simply covers the area, hampering healing and sometimes even encouraging infection. For a mild burn, application of an aloe cream or, even better, a piece of an aloe plant brings fast relief. Cold water is great for reducing inflammation.

One of the biggest problems with burns is that the defense barrier of the skin is gone. The tissues underneath the skin are exposed and vulnerable to infectious agents. On top of that, fluid loss might lead to dehydration. A dog with a large or deep burn, might need to be hospitalized for fluid therapy. Special bandages will help keep fluids in and infection out. Antibiotics are often prescribed.

Hot Dog!

In very hot weather, keep your dog quiet and cool, with plenty of fresh water and shade available. High humidity added to high temperatures is an even more deadly combination. This is no time to leave your dog in your car, which can become a fatal furnace in just a few minutes. This is also no time for those long games of fetch.

FIDO **The Doggone Truth: Normal Temperature, Heart Rate, and Respiratory Ranges**

Normal body temperatures for dogs range from 100 to 102.5 degrees Fahrenheit, normal heart rates range between 60 to 160 beats per minute, and normal respiratory rates range between 10 to 30 breaths per minute. Heart rates vary with a dog's size, age, and activity level. Hot weather and exercise can increase the breathing rate. Know what's normal for your dog!

A dog with heatstroke will pant, have trouble breathing, and might vomit or act disoriented. His heart rate might go up, and the dog could even go into seizures and die.

What to Do

Dogs sweat via their footpads and pant for temperature control. Putting ice cubes in the groin area, wiping pads with ice, and dribbling cool water in the dog's mouth might be all you need to do to help him cool off. A fan is also helpful. Just don't submerge your dog in an ice bath. Going too cold too fast can be dangerous. Try not to lower your dog's temperature below 103.5 degrees. He is safe at that temperature, and the thermometer reading will soon drop even more. If your dog has heatstroke, be sure to contact your veterinarian, even if your dog seems totally recovered.

Pupsickles

A dog who has been out in the cold too long, especially one who has been wet as well, can get hypothermia and even frostbite. Dogs with hypothermia shiver and act disoriented, and their heart rates drop. Frostbite will show up days later—usually in extremities such as ears, toes, and tail. Because these body parts don't have the extra tissue to keep them protected against the cold, they are the most common areas for frostbite. These areas might feel extremely cold, and the skin might appear white. It could be days before you know if the tissues are truly dead. If they are, they will dry up and slough off.

What to Do

Obviously, a freezing dog needs to be warmed up. Do this gradually with tepid water baths or warm towels. Dogs with frostbite might need antibiotics to prevent infection in the areas of damaged tissue.

Broken Bones

In dogs, this most often means a leg. Many times, dogs' bones get broken when a car hits them. You can tell a leg bone is broken when the leg dangles, your dog won't put any weight on it, or the bone is showing. If a car has hit your dog, take her to a veterinarian even if no bones appear to be broken. Along with obvious leg fractures, she could have broken ribs. The chances of having internal damage are high. You need to stabilize the fracture if possible.

What to Do

If your dog will lie down, gently put a paper towel tube next to the leg. Use masking tape to hold it by the leg, and then tape a towel over the whole thing. A broken leg will require a splint, cast, or surgery, using metal pins and plates to repair the damage. Do not allow a broken bone to dangle as this will cause more tissue damage.

> **Doggie Dilemmas: How Should You Carry an Injured Dog?**
> You can tuck a small dog into a towel and safely carry her in your arms. Slide a larger dog onto a blanket or board and then have two people pick him up. Either way, always take extra care if you suspect any broken bones and try not to jostle them.

Internal Damage

While broken bones are dramatic and catch our attention right away, internal damage can be more life-threatening. If your dog is having trouble breathing, is breathing very shallowly, or is coughing up blood, there's damage to the lungs and the chest. Open wounds directly into the chest are very serious.

What to Do

These are emergencies, so you must take your dog directly to the vet. Try to keep airways clear—wipe off the nose, clean anything in the mouth if you safely can. If the chest is flailing (ribs moving strangely in and out), put a wrap around the chest. Pneumothorax, the entrance of free air into the chest, can be deadly.

Abdominal Injury

While broken bones and damage to the chest and lungs are usually apparent right away, trauma injuries to the abdomen can be subtler. Although she might look fine at first glance, if your dog is bleeding internally, a check of her gums or pulse could indicate otherwise.

Any distension, or expansion, of the abdomen could indicate free blood or urine pooling in the tissues. This is cause for alarm, as is blood in the urine or stool. If your dog is suddenly apprehensive about having her abdomen touched or "splints" her abdomen (holding it very taut), you know she has pain there.

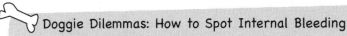

Doggie Dilemmas: How to Spot Internal Bleeding

To check for internal bleeding, first look at your dog's gums. If she has pink areas, touch them. The color should go away, then quickly come back. If the pink areas are already whitish or the color only returns slowly, she has problems. You can feel for a pulse in the groin area on the inside of a hind leg. Use your fingers (not your thumb) and you should feel a strong, steady beat.

Treating Trauma

When a dog with obvious trauma arrives at the veterinary hospital or emergency clinic, the first actions are to guard against shock. Your dog's breathing, heart rate, and temperature will quickly be checked. Direct pressure is put on any bleeding areas. An intravenous line will be placed so that fluids can be quickly injected into her system to combat shock, along with any necessary medications.

Most trauma cases will require a chest X-ray. Even a small air leak can build up over time and cause death. If there is free air in your dog's chest, a special tube will be used so that air escapes but no air gets in. The chest itself might be wrapped.

If the heart and lungs are okay, the next step is checking the abdomen. Your veterinarian might take X-rays of the abdomen as well as palpate (feel) it gently for any abnormalities. Sometimes a needle will be put into the abdomen to see if there is free fluid (urine, blood, or gastrointestinal leakage). If there seem to be any major problems in the abdomen, your dog will be stabilized before having surgery for repairs. If no major damage shows up, your dog will still probably stay overnight for careful observation.

Bloating and Swelling

As explained in Chapter 11, bloat—when a dog's stomach fills up with air and twists—is a very serious, life-threatening emergency. Bloat tends to occur in large and medium-sized breeds such as Irish setters and Great Danes, as well as some smaller breeds such as dachshunds. What many of these breeds have in common is a deep chest, which might allow more room for the stomach to move.

Experienced dog people know it's wise to rest a dog for at least an hour after a meal, allowing food to digest. It also helps to limit the amount your dog can drink right before and after a meal. Some research has investigated diet issues, such as dry food versus canned, and even certain ingredients, but there are currently no clear answers.

See the Signs

A dog with bloat might have an abdomen that looks distended. In the belly area, the skin is taut, and your dog might act as if he's in pain. Many dogs act like they are trying to vomit, but nothing comes up. Some dogs pace nervously, refusing to lie down and in general acting uncomfortable. Eventually, your dog could show signs of shock and collapse due to the changes in blood flow. A dog in shock might also have very pale gums, feel cold, and have a weak but rapid heartbeat when you feel the heart or the pulse in the groin area.

What to Do

If you suspect your dog is bloating, call your veterinarian or emergency clinic right away. When you arrive, they will quickly evaluate your dog, palpating her abdomen and listening to her heart. The next step is a stomach tube. If the tube goes in and gas is released, your dog will immediately feel more comfortable. If the tube can't get into the stomach due to a twist, your veterinarian might stick a large needle right through the body wall into the distended stomach to relieve pressure and release some gas. Your dog will then head into surgery if her heart is stable.

The Doggone Truth: The Effects of Bloat

If your dog's stomach has been twisted for a long time, or is twisted very tightly, some tissue will be necrotic (dead) due to reduced blood flow. This is dangerous, as untwisting the tissues will release nasty bacteria and toxins. While your veterinarian will try to reduce the effects of those toxins with medications, some dogs do not survive. Other dogs will require removal of the dead tissues.

In surgery, the stomach is carefully untwisted, and the intestines and stomach are carefully evaluated for damage. The stomach is then fastened down to the body wall with sutures in an effort to prevent a recurrence of the problem. Most dogs end up staying in the hospital for a couple of days with intravenous fluids and careful observation.

Seizures

It's important to know which quick first-aid techniques you can apply to your dog in case of a seizure. Seizures are like short circuits in the electricity of your dog's brain. With no conscious control, your dog can stagger, twitch, vocalize, and even urinate or defecate. This is scary, but you need to stay calm and help your dog. Most dogs show distinct "pre-ictal" or preseizure behaviors. They might become very clingy, pacing and acting uncomfortable, and some go off to a safe hiding place. If your dog has epilepsy, you will usually be able to detect a pattern to the seizures.

Old Seizure Myths

Dogs can't swallow their tongues, so don't stick your hand in the mouth of a seizuring dog to grab the tongue. You'll just end up getting bitten. The best way to help your dog is to guide her gently to a safe place, away from stairs she could fall down or other things she could bang into, and comfort her. Most dogs respond to being held in a blanket and to soothing touch and talk. Seizures generally last less than five minutes, even though it feels like forever to you!

 The Doggone Truth: What Causes Seizures?
The most common cause of seizures or epilepsy in dogs is genetic predisposition. Seizures can also be a result of metabolic problems like low blood sugar, cancer, infection, or trauma.

Recovery

As your dog comes out of the seizure, she might be disoriented. Calmly clean her up if need be. She might need to be gently restrained, as some dogs have vision problems right after a seizure. Dogs are usually back to 100 percent in an hour or two, and some are normal in minutes.

If your dog seizures for more than five minutes or has repeated seizures, call your veterinarian. Prolonged seizures can raise the body's temperature to dangerous levels. "Status seizures," seizures that repeat quickly or continue on for long periods, can do permanent damage to your dog's brain cells or even kill her.

If this is your dog's first seizure, you should also contact your veterinarian. Your veterinarian will do a thorough exam and look for causes of the seizures, by doing blood work to check out her liver function and look for any signs of poisoning, toxins, or infections. At some point X-rays or an electroencephalogram might be needed. You will need to discuss with your veterinarian whether your dog needs to start treatments. All medications have side effects. If your dog only seizures once a year, she might be better off without daily medications.

Mark your calendar any time your dog has a seizure (or even if you suspect she might have had one while you were out). Eventually you might be able to predict when the seizures will come and give your dog extra medication.

FIDO The Doggone Truth: Unusual Behaviors Could Indicate Seizures

It's now thought that some obsessive-compulsive behaviors, such as intense tail chasing, and some instances when dogs suddenly act aggressively might actually be seizure disorders. If your dog shows these symptoms, see a veterinary behaviorist.

What to Do

Unless your dog has seizures from a well-known cause, such as a liver problem that can be treated, you need to assume your treatment goal will be to minimize the number and length of any seizures, not to cure your dog. Luckily, some dogs respond extremely well to seizure treatments. Part of the care for seizuring dogs involves being very careful about diet, exercise, and anything that might stimulate a seizure. Work with your veterinarian to design a lifestyle plan customized for your dog.

Medications are an important part of controlling seizures. Phenobarbital and potassium bromide are the best-known medications for dogs. Liver problems can be a side effect so your veterinarian might also prescribe herbal medications such as milk thistle to minimize those reactions. Diazepam (valium) is often used to help stop a seizure, and your veterinarian might provide you with a diazepam enema to give at home if needed. Once your dog starts on seizure medications, you must be faithful, giving the medications daily and on a routine schedule. Suddenly stopping medications might precipitate more seizures.

Heart Problems

While dogs do not normally suffer the classic heart attacks we see in people, canines can have heart conditions that cause acute collapse. Dilated cardiomyopathy is a disease with an inherited predisposition in some breeds such as Doberman pinschers and boxers. In this case, the heart ("cardio") muscle ("myo") is stretched and thinned out so much it can no longer efficiently pump the right amount of blood. The body receives less oxygenated blood than it needs, and areas get shut down, leading to collapse.

If caught early, by noticing less stamina or labored breathing, or on a routine exam by your veterinarian, this condition can be controlled for a while with medications. Unfortunately, though, the only real cure is a heart transplant, which isn't available for dogs.

Atrial and ventricular fibrillation, in which the small atrial or larger ventricular chambers of the heart beat so fast they don't actually move much blood, can also lead to acute collapse. This can be caused by damage to the heart muscle or the nerves controlling the heart rate or by stimulating toxins. This condition can be diagnosed in a routine exam, or you might notice your dog's lack of energy and stamina, coupled often with panting or pacing.

Lack of Oxygen

Along with the heart failing to pump enough oxygenated blood, your dog might actually not be getting enough oxygen into his lungs. Even something as simple as getting a tennis ball stuck in his mouth can block a dog's airways and cause him to collapse. In this case, you must quickly pull that obstruction out.

Dogs with short faces—such as English and French bulldogs—might suffer from brachycephalic syndrome, especially in hot, humid weather. These breeds often have small nasal openings and a long soft palate (flap on the roof of the mouth). When a dog breathes, air is pulled in, creating some negative pressure inside the palate. In these dogs, the palate can get sucked down and block off the airways. This could lead to a faint or collapse.

What to Do

If your short-faced dog labors to breathe in hot, humid weather, ask your veterinarian to do a thorough airway exam (possibly under anesthesia). Surgery might be required to help these dogs breathe easily.

Neurological Problems

A dog with a sudden injury to the discs in the neck or back, or with chronic degeneration of these discs, might collapse and even be paralyzed. In these situations, the protective shock-absorbing disc in between two vertebrae has been squeezed and is putting pressure directly on the spinal cord. Depending on exactly where this happens, your dog might be in great pain, lose control of his hind end, or even lose control of most of his body. Long-backed dogs such as dachshunds and Bassets tend to have problems with disc disease. Great Danes and Doberman pinschers have neck disc problems.

Electrical Shocks

An electrical shock can be deadly or merely spine tingling, depending on just how much power coursed through your dog's body. Most dogs get electrical shocks by chewing on electric cords. When puppy-proofing your home, run wires through rubber or plastic hose or arrange wires

first aid for your furry friend

where your curious canine can't reach them. Even an older dog might grab a wire if it runs across his path. A quick bite might leave your dog with just a slightly sore mouth, but a definite grab could give his mouth an electrical burn (visible on the corners of the lips and on the tongue) or even disrupt the electrical patterns of his heart, leading to collapse.

What to Do

The first and most important thing to remember is that if you get shocked too, you won't be able to help your dog. Use a piece of wood, like a broomstick, to snatch the plug from the wall. If necessary, flip the circuit breakers to shut off power to the area.

Electric shocks can also happen outside the home. A sparking wire on the ground, especially if it is wet out, can present grave danger to both you and your dog. If your dog collapses near a downed wire, stay clear to keep yourself protected. Use a tree branch or long wooden pole to slide the wire away from your dog or your dog away from the wire. If this is impossible or too dangerous, give your utility company an emergency alert call.

Once your dog is safely away from the electrical danger, check her heartbeat and see if she's breathing. If need be, administer CPR. Even if your dog comes around quickly, go to your veterinarian for a thorough exam. Sometimes problems show up a day or so later.

Chapter 14

As Your Dog Ages

 ASK MOST PEOPLE, and they'd probably tell you that the biggest drawback to having a dog is they don't live nearly as long as we'd like them to. Depending on breed, diet, and overall health, the average dog lives to be about twelve years old. Giant breeds tend to have shorter life spans of eight to ten years, while smaller breeds sometimes live into their late teens. Even if we can't keep the dogs we love so much with us forever, there are still things we can do to help them live longer and ensure their quality of life, thanks to advances in nutrition and veterinary care. Simply by providing the right exercise, adjusting his diet as needed, and taking your dog for regular veterinary exams can help your dog live to a healthy, happy, and ripe old age.

Signs of Seniority

It's often said that seven years is the age that marks the beginning of the senior years for dogs. In reality, individual dogs age at different rates, just like people. Lots of dogs are still going strong and looking young at seven and beyond, while others do indeed live up to this stereotype. Here are some signs that your dog might be getting old:

- ❧ Graying of the muzzle and eyebrows
- ❧ A thinning coat
- ❧ A drop in energy level
- ❧ Weight gain or weight loss
- ❧ More frequent urination

Older dogs also tend to move more slowly because of stiff or painful joints. The lens of their eye becomes hazy, which is a normal part of aging, or it's sometimes clouded with cataracts. Teeth become looser and more tartar-encrusted if good dental hygiene isn't practiced. Older dogs are also sometimes less able to tolerate extremely hot or cold weather.

Geriatric Exams

If your young-at-heart dog suddenly starts acting old, it's definitely time to schedule a checkup. He might have a health problem that needs to be dealt with—fast! But even if your dog still acts like a youngster, it's a good idea to schedule a geriatric screening exam once he hits his seventh birthday. This exam checks a number of key health considerations—weight, dental health, blood chemistry, and so on—so you and your vet can establish a baseline for comparison as your dog ages. By screening for age-related health problems at this early stage, you're more likely to uncover health issues while they can still be dealt with easily.

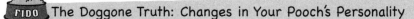

FIDO **The Doggone Truth: Changes in Your Pooch's Personality**

Besides physical changes, your dog might start to show some behavioral changes as well. She might sleep more or be less attentive. Her sense of smell might become less acute—prompting your once-voracious canine to have less of an appetite. As your dog ages, remember it's also important to give her a stable routine. This helps reduce stress, which is tougher on old dogs than on young ones.

Besides checking your dog for obvious physical signs of aging such as stiffness, heart murmurs, bad breath, and skin lesions, a complete geriatric exam includes blood work, urinalysis, and other diagnostic tests to assess liver and kidney function, check for anemia or hidden infections, and otherwise examine body chemistry.

Eating Right

Puppies aren't the only ones who have special nutritional needs—so do older dogs. Because they're less active, they don't need as many calories to maintain a healthy weight. They do, however, need a high-quality protein food to make up for the digestive system's decreased ability to efficiently metabolize protein.

The best food for an older dog contains about 25 percent protein and has a lower concentration of fat and calories than a regular dog food. Some diets formulated for older dogs—or for dogs that need to lose weight—are high in fiber, which helps reduce caloric density. A

as your dog ages

223

dog eating this type of diet will feel full, even though he's not getting as many calories.

Special Diets

Many health problems and some cancers can be managed with a special diet. Some special diets contain ingredients believed to promote joint health, which can be beneficial for older dogs. At least one food marketed for older dogs contains antioxidants and other nutrients that might help fight the signs of brain aging or age-related behavioral changes. These types of foods are available only by prescription from your veterinarian. If your older dog has a health problem, ask if a change in diet will help.

Doggie Dilemmas: Does My Dog Need Vitamin Supplements?

Most veterinary nutritionists agree that a dog fed a balanced diet doesn't need supplements. When it comes to an older dog, though, some supplements can be beneficial. For instance, dogs with reduced kidney function might need a B vitamin. And for dogs with dry, itchy skin, adding vitamin E, zinc, or essential fatty acids to the diet might help. Ask your veterinarian if supplements could be helpful for your older dog.

Not So Hungry?

Older dogs often begin to eat less. Their teeth might hurt or their sense of smell—which is linked to the ability to taste—might be reduced. Tartar buildup on teeth can cause pain, so consider taking your dog in for a veterinary cleaning if you notice lots of brown buildup on his teeth. You might be amazed when he starts acting like a puppy again because he's feeling so much better. If tartar buildup isn't the problem, try warming his food in the microwave before serving it. The heat increases the scent, making it easier for him to realize that there's a yummy meal sitting in front of him. (This works for dry food as well as canned.) Don't forget to test the food for hot spots with your finger before serving.

Be concerned if you try these tricks and your dog still doesn't have much of an appetite. That means it's time for a vet checkup. He might have a hidden health problem, especially if he's rapidly losing weight.

Going Up or Down?

Pay attention if your dog suddenly starts gaining or losing weight. Both can be signs of an underlying health problem. If your dog is gaining weight, look at the amount of food you're giving him as well as the amount of exercise he gets. It's all too easy to slack off on walking or playing with an older dog, especially if he doesn't seem interested.

If you're still feeding him the same amount he was getting when he was younger and more active, well, no wonder he's putting on weight. Unexplained weight gain can also be related to certain health conditions, such as hypothyroidism.

As for weight loss: If your dog eats ravenously but still loses weight, he might have diabetes. Picking up food and then dropping it can mean that your dog's teeth hurt. Weight loss can also be an early, subtle sign of cancer. Whether your dog is gaining or losing weight, take him to the veterinarian to rule out any health problems.

FIDO The Doggone Truth: Health Problems in Older Dogs

There's no getting around it. No matter how well you take care of him, your dog will eventually experience some of the aches and pains that go along with old age. While the details on various problems in the sections that follow might seem overwhelming, the good news is that veterinarians now have more and better ways of treating them, especially when they're caught early.

Arthritis

At last count, more than 8 million dogs in the United States had been diagnosed with this painful degenerative joint disease, and more than 80 percent of them were seven years or older. Dogs with arthritis usually show the following signs:

- Stiffness when getting up or lying down
- Lowered activity level
- Reluctance to walk very far or to climb stairs
- Flinching or snapping when touched
- Swollen joints that seem hot or painful

Arthritis doesn't have a cure, but a number of medications are available to relieve the pain of achy-breaky joints.

Medications for Arthritis

Your veterinarian can prescribe a nonsteroidal anti-inflammatory drug (NSAID) to relieve pain and inflammation. These drugs are similar to the ibuprofen or acetaminophen you might take for yourself, but they're formulated specifically for dogs. Remember, your ibuprofen or other NSAID can be toxic to your dog, so never give him anything like that without your veterinarian's okay. Canine NSAIDs are generally safe, but they can have side effects—vomiting, diarrhea, and liver or kidney damage—and some dogs (Labs in particular) are highly sensitive to them. Your veterinarian might need to adjust the dose or try a different drug if your dog has problems. She will probably also require periodic blood work to check liver and kidney values before renewing a prescription.

Other Types of Pain Relief

If you have a small dog, lift him on and off furniture throughout his life, but especially as he gets older. This helps prevent cumulative joint damage. Keep your dog's weight at a healthy level to reduce stress on the joints. And think about pampering your pooch with a heated bed. Warmth is one of the best ways to relieve joint pain.

Cancer

Cancer occurs when cells grow uncontrollably on or inside the body. The risk of cancer increases with age, and common cancers seen in dogs include mammary (breast) tumors, skin tumors, testicular tumors (in unneutered males), mouth cancer, and lymphoma. Be concerned about cancer if your dog shows any of the following signs:

- ❧ Lumps that don't go away or that grow larger
- ❧ Sores that don't heal
- ❧ Unusual or excessive weight loss
- ❧ Lack of appetite for more than a day or two
- ❧ Bleeding or discharge from any body opening
- ❧ Difficulty eating or swallowing
- ❧ Unexplained lack of energy

Veterinarians generally diagnose cancer with a biopsy, the removal and study of a section of tissue. Your vet might also use blood work and X-rays for diagnosis.

Breast Cancer

Mammary tumors are the most common type of cancer in female dogs and are most often seen in older unspayed females. The tumors can be removed surgically, and your dog might also need chemotherapy afterward. The best way to prevent or greatly reduce the risk of mammary cancer is to spay a female before her first heat cycle.

Skin Cancer

It's not unusual for older dogs to develop lumps and bumps on or beneath their skin. Generally these growths are harmless, but it's a good idea to have your veterinarian take a look to be sure. Always take your dog in for a checkup if a growth becomes larger or changes color.

Canine Quick Fix: Removing Harmless Growths

Harmless but unsightly growths such as cysts, papillomas (warts), adenomas, and lipomas can be removed surgically. This might be a particularly good idea if a growth is impeding your dog's movement.

Mast cell tumors are a common type of malignant skin cancer. They can develop anywhere on or in the body and resemble raised, nodular masses. Mast cell tumors can feel solid or soft when touched. Most commonly, they develop in dogs who are eight to ten years old, although they can occur at any age. The best treatment is surgical removal, sometimes followed by radiation. In advanced stages of the disease, chemotherapy might be helpful.

Testicular Cancer

Testicular tumors usually develop in male dogs that are at least ten years old, but they have occurred in dogs as young as three. Dogs with retained testicles (which remain up inside the body) are most likely to develop testicular cancer. Testicular cancer is treated surgically, followed by chemotherapy or radiation if the tumor has spread. You can avoid this problem by having your dog neutered.

Mouth Cancer

The most common mouth (oral) cancer in dogs is malignant melanoma. One out of every twenty canine cancer diagnoses is for this disease. Malignant melanoma is highly aggressive, so catching it early is important. That's just one of the many good reasons for brushing your dog's teeth on a regular basis—you're more likely to spot the signs of this disease, which include a mass on the gums, bleeding gums, bad breath, or difficulty eating.

FIDO The Doggone Truth: Canine Chemotherapy

Luckily, dogs don't suffer the same side effects from chemotherapy that people do. Your dog won't lose his hair or become nauseous, but you might notice he's tired for a few days after each treatment.

Oral cancers are diagnosed with biopsies and X-rays. They're treated surgically, although radiation therapy might be needed as a follow-up. Also, a DNA-based vaccine is currently being studied at New York City's Animal Medical Center as an alternative treatment.

Lymphoma

If your dog has an unusual swelling or enlargement in the lower neck area, he might have lymphoma, a tumor of the blood-forming system. A vet exam might show that all the body's lymph nodes are enlarged. Blood work, a biopsy, and chest and abdominal X-rays could be necessary to confirm the diagnosis and determine where the tumor is located and how large it is. Lymphoma usually responds well to chemotherapy.

Canine Senility

We all use the term "senility" loosely and generally know what it means. But more specifically, senility—formally known as cognitive dysfunction syndrome (CDS)—is an age-related mental decline not caused by hearing or vision loss, organ failure, or cancer. Senile dogs might wander aimlessly, act confused or disoriented, stare into space, change their activity or sleep habits, or withdraw from family members. Dogs can show signs of CDS as early as eight years of age.

If you think your dog has CDS, don't assume nothing can be done. Take him to the veterinarian for a definitive diagnosis first, to rule out health problems that can mimic CDS. These include kidney, thyroid, or adrenal gland disease. Then ask your veterinarian about medication that can help. You might also want to give your dog choline supplements, which are believed to help increase mental alertness. These supplements are available at holistic veterinary clinics, pet supply stores, online pet supply stores, and health food stores.

Congestive Heart Failure

When the heart is too weak to pump blood adequately, fluid accumulates in the lungs, causing a condition known as congestive heart failure (CHF). Your dog might have CHF if he coughs frequently, has trouble breathing, seems restless at night, or tires easily after mild exercise. It's most common in old, overweight dogs. There's no cure for CHF, but it can be managed for a time with diet, medication, and rest. Weight loss helps, too.

Teeth Issues

Most older dogs develop some dental disease, especially toy breeds with a mouth full of crowded teeth. But teeth problems are easy to prevent—all it takes is brushing daily. Remember, good dental health is related to good overall health. When dental disease goes untreated, the mouth becomes a breeding ground for bacteria, which then enter the bloodstream and go throughout the body.

That said, some dogs just plain have bad teeth and will develop plaque and tartar no matter how much you brush. Take them in for veterinary cleanings annually to keep their mouth in good shape.

Diabetes

Diabetes is a common problem in older dogs, especially if they're overweight or have a genetic predisposition to the disease, as some breeds do. It's a disorder of the pancreas gland and develops when the pancreas doesn't produce enough insulin—the substance the body uses to drive glucose, or blood sugar, into the cells—or stops producing insulin altogether. When this happens, glucose levels build up in the bloodstream instead of being used for energy. Certain breeds have a tendency for diabetes, including golden and Labrador retrievers, German shepherds, keeshonds, poodles, and pugs.

Diagnosing Diabetes

Your dog might have diabetes if he suddenly seems thirsty all the time and starts needing to urinate much more often. He might even have accidents in the house. Dogs with diabetes often have a ravenous appetite, but they lose weight despite eating everything they can find. If the disease goes long enough without a diagnosis, dogs might even go blind. If your dog shows any of these signs, take him in for blood work and a urinalysis.

Managing Diabetes

There's no cure for diabetes, but it can be managed with daily insulin injections and diet. Establishing the right amount of insulin for your dog involves some trial and error. Your veterinarian can show you how to give the injection. With a little practice it's easy. Most dogs don't seem to mind the injection, especially if you give them a treat or a meal immediately afterward. Dogs with diabetes need a diet full of good quality protein and some extra fiber to stabilize blood sugar levels. Such diets can be prepared at home, but your veterinarian might prefer to prescribe a commercial diabetes diet for your dog. Weight loss through exercise and diet is also important in managing the disease. Your dog will need periodic blood work to assess his status.

Hearing Loss

Don't assume your old dog is ignoring you when you call him to come and he doesn't respond. The poor fella could be a bit hard of hearing. As dogs age, they experience degenerative changes in the inner ear and a stiffening of the eardrum, and their hearing becomes less acute because of that.

How Do You Know It's Deafness?

If you suspect your dog isn't hearing so well anymore, try this test. Walk up behind him and make a noise by clapping your hands or dropping your keys. If he doesn't jump up and whirl around in response, he might well have partial or total hearing loss. Your veterinarian can confirm the diagnosis of deafness and make sure that it's not caused by a treatable condition such as an ear infection or neurological disease.

Living with a Deaf Dog

If your dog is deaf, there are some simple adjustments you can make to help you communicate just fine with him. To let him know you're behind him, stomp your foot. He'll feel the vibrations and know where you are.

This is definitely the time to make good use of those hand signals you learned in obedience class. Many dogs respond better to hand signals than to verbal commands anyway. As for your dog, he'll simply make more use of his senses of sight and smell.

You might also think about getting your dog a canine hearing aid. Don't laugh, they really are available. If you have pet health insurance, check to see if your plan covers hearing aids, which cost about $400. Keep in mind, however, that dog hearing aids can fall out easily, so they might get lost.

Canine Quick Fix: Practice Those Hand Signals

If your dog is still a puppy as you're reading this, start teaching him hand signals now. They'll come in handy, so to speak, for communication throughout his life, not only if he has hearing difficulties. Two basic hand signals are a rising hand for sit and a raised hand, palm out, for wait or stay.

Hypothyroidism

Hypothyroidism is a decrease in thyroid function. It's the most common hormonal disorder seen in dogs and usually develops in dogs that are middle-aged or older. If your dog's level of thyroid hormones falls below normal, you'll see such signs as rough, scaly skin or skin infections; hair loss on both sides of the body or the rear end; and weight gain for no apparent reason. To diagnose hypothyroidism, your veterinarian will run blood work to check the levels of circulating thyroid hormones (T3 and T4).

A daily dose of synthetic thyroid hormone, which is available in the form of a chewable tablet, is used to manage hypothyroidism. The amount your dog needs depends on how much he weighs. Your veterinarian will recommend blood work every six months to make sure the dose doesn't need to be adjusted.

Kidney Disease

Kidney disease is one of the most common problems in old dogs, second only to cancer. As the kidneys age, they become less efficient at removing waste products from the body, causing waste to build up instead of being eliminated with urine. A new screening test allows veterinarians to identify kidney disease in the early stages, when it's still possible to manage it with a special low-protein diet that won't overwork the kidneys. Your dog can live significantly longer if kidney disease is caught and managed early—another good reason for regular screening exams.

Sight Issues

Nuclear sclerosis and cataracts are two common vision problems in aging dogs. If the center of your dog's eye lens appears hazy or gray, he has nuclear sclerosis—a normal part of the eye's aging process. Nuclear sclerosis is caused by the formation of new fibers at the edge of the lens. These fibers push inward toward the center. Nuclear sclerosis isn't painful and it won't greatly affect your dog's vision, although he might have a little trouble focusing on objects close-up.

Acquired cataracts—as opposed to juvenile cataracts, which are congenital or hereditary—are generally a consequence of aging or a side effect of diabetes. Cataracts cause the lens to become opaque, starting at the center of the lens and spreading outward, gradually decreasing vision. Fortunately, dogs who are blind or have limited vision can get around quite well using their senses of smell and hearing. You can also learn to communicate with them using a whistle. Consult a trainer for advice on how to do this.

Canine Quick Fix: Scenting Objects

Cataracts can sometimes be removed surgically, but if that's not possible, help your dog navigate his surroundings by scenting furniture and other objects at his nose level. Just be sure to test an inconspicuous area first to make sure that the perfume or other scent you use doesn't harm the finish.

Comfy Living

There are lots of simple things you can do to keep your pooch comfortable as he gets older.

- Put soft bedding in his favorite places so he always has a comfy place to rest.
- Get him a heated bed; the warmth will soothe old bones and painful joints.
- Lift him on and off furniture to protect his joints.
- Build him a ramp up to the bed, sofa, or car so he doesn't have to jump up.
- Install a dog door so he can go potty outside as often as necessary, or take him out more often.
- Keep a thin-coated dog warm during winter with a sweater, as old dogs are more sensitive to temperature extremes.
- Take him on short, easy walks every day to keep his blood flowing and his joints moving.
- Brush his teeth and schedule regular veterinary cleanings.
- Check him for lumps, bumps, or sores as you groom him.

Try these things, and your dog is sure to be happy in his golden years!

When It's Time to Say Goodbye

It's never easy to know when the time is right to let your dog go, but it can help to look at his overall quality of life. This means honestly evaluating his appetite, attitude, activity level, comfort, elimination habits, and interaction with people, especially family members. Ask yourself the following questions:

- ❧ Does my dog have more good days than bad?
- ❧ Can he still do his favorite things?
- ❧ Is he still capable of controlling his urination and defecation?
- ❧ Does he still like to eat?
- ❧ Does he act as if he's in pain more often than not?
- ❧ Does he still enjoy being petted and talked to?

If you answer no to the majority of these questions, it's time to talk to your veterinarian about euthanasia. Although it's difficult to face, sometimes a dog is so sick, old, or severely injured that he will never recover normal health. When this is the case, the kindest thing you can do is to give him a quiet, humane death. Because you know your dog best, this is a decision only you can make. Still, consulting your veterinarian and other family members will help.

Veterinarians love animals, so they understand how difficult making the decision to euthanize a favorite pet can be. Although she can't make the decision for you, your veterinarian can help guide you by fully explaining your dog's condition, his chances for recovery, and his long-term prognosis. Armed with this information, you can make the decision that's right for you and your dog.

Honoring Your Dog

For thousands of years, people have accorded dogs the same rites of death they had for themselves. Dogs have been found in graves buried with people, and the Egyptians mummified dogs so they would be with them in the afterlife. Today, there are several options for honoring your dog after his death. He can be cremated or buried in a pet cemetery or, sometimes, on your own property. (There are other alternatives as well, including having your dog's ashes transformed into a diamond.)

Pet Cemeteries

Among the first pet cemeteries of the modern era were Asnieres, near Paris, and Hartsdale Canine Cemetery, in New York, founded in 1896, the oldest pet cemetery in the United States. Today, there are more than 600 pet cemeteries in the United States. The largest U.S. pet cemetery is Bide-a-Wee Home Association, located in New York.

You can find a pet cemetery in your area by contacting the International Association of Pet Cemeteries (*www.iaopc.com*).

Choose a cemetery that's located on land the proprietors own. Check to see that the cemetery is deeded to prevent future land development or other non-cemetery use of the property. The cemetery should also maintain a care fund to ensure that funds will be available to maintain the grounds.

Most pet cemeteries have a transport service and will pick up your dog's body from your home or from your veterinarian's office. They offer cremation or burial and can work with you to choose an urn, headstone, and burial site. The costs for cemetery burial vary. You can choose communal burial, communal cremation, or individual burial or cremation. (Communal cremation is the least expensive option; individual burial is the most expensive.)

FIDO **The Doggone Truth: Don't Hide This Decision from Your Kids**
If you have children, it's important to involve them in the euthanasia decision. Even if they aren't old enough to understand all the implications, you can still explain your dog is very sick and the veterinarian can't make him better. It helps to let children talk it out. Give honest, simple answers to their questions. And avoid using the phrase "putting the dog to sleep." This can scare young children and make them afraid to go to bed at night.

If you do decide to cremate your dog, you can store the ashes in an urn and have them placed in a columbarium at the cemetery, but you can also keep them at home in a pretty urn or box, or scatter them in your dog's favorite place.

Burying Your Dog at Home

Burying your dog at home is certainly less expensive and it allows you to visit your dog's resting place at any time, but it does have some drawbacks. Unless you plan to be in the same home for the rest of your life, you'll have to leave your dog's body behind when you move. You must also consider local or county ordinances or state laws that regulate pet burial. Then there's the concern that other animals might try to dig up your pet's remains. Your veterinarian or the local pet cemetery might be able to advise you on the legalities, or you can check with your municipal government.

If you bury your dog at home, place him in a nonbiodegradable container. You can purchase a wooden casket from a pet cemetery or use some other wood or metal container. Before you put the body in the casket, place it in a heavy-duty plastic bag. Bury the receptacle at least three feet deep, to prevent other animals from digging up the grave. You can plant a tree, some perennial flowers (which bloom year after year), or another favorite plant at the site, or you can mark it with a plaque or headstone.

Dealing with Grief

People often feel embarrassed about grieving for a dog, but the loss of any special relationship is devastating, especially if it's one that has lasted many years. Never be ashamed of crying or otherwise expressing sorrow over your loss. Don't be surprised if you find yourself bursting into tears for days or even weeks after your dog's death. It's not something you can control—unless you just want to walk around with a big lump in your throat all the time. Let yourself cry. It's part of the healing process. Your true friends and anyone who loves animals will understand.

If you have children, you'll need to help them to deal with their grief even as you are trying to cope with your own. Children are more open about expressing their feelings than adults, and this can be helpful when it comes to dealing with grief.

Young children up to the age of five tend to have what is called magical thinking. They're still not quite clear on the differences between reality and make-believe. Give them concrete explanations about your dog's death. Assure your child that your dog died without pain and now doesn't hurt anymore. Encourage her to write a story about the dog or draw a picture of him. Writing and art are good therapy!

Rituals are important to older children. Let them help pick out where to bury your dog or a photo to have framed. They might want to lead the family on a walk to your dog's favorite places.

Fitting Tributes

Doing something good for other dogs, or establishing a ritual to remember your dog might help to ease your grief. Making a donation in your dog's name to a shelter or to support veterinary research is a concrete way of ensuring your dog's life stands for something. Lighting a candle on the anniversary of his birth or death, or choosing a specific day (such as November 1, which is celebrated as All Saints Day or Day of the Dead in some cultures) to remember all past pets helps focus your attention on memories of your dog. And a plant or a photo album provides a visual reminder of the good times. Although you might not believe it at the time when your grief is so fresh, someday, when you are ready, you will get another dog. And this is the best tribute you could ever give to your best friend, because you'll be helping another wonderful animal by giving her a loving home. A new dog will never replace your previous dog, but trust us—your heart really is big enough to love and care for any number of special dogs.

Index